Who the Hell is David Hume?

Who the Hell is David Hume?

And what are his theories all about?

Dr Mark Robson

BOWDEN
&BRAZIL

First published in Great Britain in 2020 by
Bowden & Brazil Ltd
Felixstowe, Suffolk, UK.

ISBN 978-1-9999492-5-9

To find out more about other books and authors in this series,
visit www.whothehellis.co.uk

Contents

Introduction

Hume is almost universally acknowledged to be the greatest British philosopher of all time. The mark of greatness in any discipline is originality and Hume has that in abundance. His thoughts about causation, religion, morality, psychology (amongst others) are all deeply insightful and he sees new problems and asks new questions in all these areas. For example, the problem of induction that we examine in Chapter 3 is a problem that Hume was the first to see. No one else had really understood that a foundational cornerstone of all our thinking in science, and in everyday life, is bereft of a proper justification.

Hume's ideas and arguments have all had a deep impact upon the thinking of the Western world, and surprising connections to Eastern philosophies (see Murti, 1960 and Gopnik, 2009). If someone wants to understand contemporary culture and thinking, they need to understand Hume's ideas. It can sometimes seem as though the ways of thinking that hold sway in a culture are inevitable, and that people have always thought these ways. It can seem that we have eternally wandered these particular intellectual byroads and avenues. But that is not so. Philosophers change the world and its thinking. New land is sighted. New roads are built, and Hume is one of the most prolific of road builders.

Naturally enough Hume's thinking emerges from a tradition. His empiricism comes from a rich vein of thought that sees experience as central to human knowledge. Philosophers such as William of Ockham, Francis Bacon and Thomas Hobbes had insisted on the minute and careful examination of experience. British empiricism gave new impetus to scientific endeavours and is itself, in turn, deeply influenced by science. Hume's deep contribution to this tradition has influenced a whole host of modern philosophers, and Hume's thoughts have embedded themselves into our culture.

The so-called 'New Atheism', espoused by eminent thinkers today such as Daniel Dennett, Christopher Hitchens, Sam Harris and Richard Dawkins, has Hume as its great ancestor. When they argue that religion is due to our anthropomorphising of the environment, they are speaking in Humean language. Hume claims that the origin of religious thought lies in the fear of natural disaster, and our subsequent desperate desire to rationalize this as the work of some divine mind. If it is a mind, then, perhaps there is some purpose behind the apparent chaos of flood, earthquake and disease. Religion, according to this way of viewing, is little more than a mental comfort blanket, an unwarranted casting of a human face upon the inanimate.

Despite Hume's confidence in his pronouncements about the origin of religion, his thinking was ultimately sceptical. Having dismissed the idea that reason alone could show us truths about the world, he was disappointed to find that experience did not prove to be the fount of knowledge either. He seemed to despair of this in his early work, *A Treatise of Human Nature* (1739–40), but rallied later in life seeing doubt and scepticism as a useful antidote to excessive enthusiasm and trenchant opinion. Doubt can be the great ameliorator since it can calm the passions.

This scepticism inspired the greatest of modern philosophers, the Prussian German Immanuel Kant, to try to clear away the doubt. Kant says that Hume awoke him from his 'dogmatic slumbers'. It certainly did. In the 1780s Kant produced what is probably the most prolific output of philosophical insight the world has ever known.

Hume, then, needs to be read and understood. To do so, is to embark upon an intellectual adventure of the profoundest kind.

1. Hume's Life Story

David Hume was born in Edinburgh, Scotland on 26 April 1711, the third and final child of Joseph Home and Katherine Falconer. The family name was Home, but Hume changed the spelling in 1734 in order to mark its pronunciation better (it was actually pronounced 'Hume' in the Scottish tongue). His father, Joseph, was the laird of Ninewells, a small farming estate near the English–Scottish borders, and his mother, Katherine, was the daughter of Sir David Falconer, Lord President of the Court of Session (Scotland's supreme court). The family were reasonably prosperous, but in 1713 Joseph died at the age of 33, leaving Katherine in sole care of three children under five years old. In his short autobiography, *My Own Life*, Hume describes his mother as 'a woman of singular merit, who, though young and handsome, devoted herself entirely to the rearing and educating of her children' (Hume 1776).

Little is known about Hume's siblings, John and Katherine, apart from a description of John by the writer James Boswell, who met John in 1762 and noted that he had 'an anxiety of temper which hurts him. Very different from his brother'. During the seven years following his father's death, little is known about the young Hume, though his later admission to university suggests that the family followed the norm and employed tutors for the children to learn to read and write English, and probably Latin.

University and Despair

Hume went to Edinburgh university at the age of 10 which was younger than usual, but still fairly unremarkable at the time. It is probable that he went at such a young age because it was thought appropriate for him to go at the same time as his older brother, John, who was 12 years old.

In those days, universities were very different institutions than today. One scholar describes the mission of education at the time as being 'to train students for virtuous living in a society regulated by religious observance' (Stewart, 2005). Hume would have studied Latin, Greek, logic and metaphysics, and he would have had lectures in natural philosophy (or, as we would call it,

Fig. 1 Edinburgh University, founded in 1582, is one of the oldest universities in the UK.

science). Much of the work was little more than rote learning with question-and-answer style course notes generously peppered with religious examples. There seems to have been little room for questioning of authority or rebellion against the status quo.

One of Hume's professors, Colin Drummond, justified the fees paid to the lecturers as due payment for the old and wise imparting knowledge to the young and stupid. He wrote,

> *'The talented in every age have derived payment for their pains in transmitting certain rules and precepts by which deficiencies in knowledge, and errors in the knowledge of things, may be uncovered and thereby avoided and corrected.'* (Stewart, 2005)

It appears that universities existed mainly to quell radical thinking, rather than stimulate it. Their purpose was to instil certain values and learning – certainly not to nurture the kind of sceptical questioning for which Hume would become famous. It is little wonder that Hume would say in 1735 that he could 'see no reason why we shou'd either go to a University, more than to any other place, or trouble ourselves about the Learning or Capacity of a Professor'. Indeed, he later told a friend that 'there is nothing to be learnt from a Professor, which is not to be met with in books'.

However, from an early age Hume was not satisfied with the mere rote learning of catechisms and other exercises. He chose instead to nourish his mind with independent reading. In a short biographical essay, titled *My Own Life* (1776) he records being 'seized very early with a passion for literature, which has been the ruling passion of my life, and the great source of my enjoyments'.

Elsewhere, in 'Letter to a Physician' (quoted in Greig, 1932) he writes that 'from my earliest infancy, I found always a strong inclination to books and letters', but never as a passive reader; he continues: 'Upon examination [of various works] I found a certain boldness of temper growing in me, which was not inclined to submit to any authority in these subjects'.

We do not know in exact detail what Hume studied. The professions that he might have considered, as befitting his family status, included the clergy (which his lack of faith precluded) and the law. He notes in his short biography (1776) that he did study the law for a short while at the age of 17, but abruptly ended it.

> *'My studious disposition, my sobriety, and my industry, gave my family a notion that the law was a proper profession for me; but I found an insurmountable aversion to everything but the pursuits of philosophy and general learning; and while they fancied I was poring upon Voet and Vinnius, Cicero and Virgil were the authors which I was secretly devouring.'*

The burning drive with which Hume applied himself to studying seems to have led to some kind of burn-out – Hume describes himself as 'being a little broken by my ardent application' (Hume, 1776). In 'Letter to a Physician', he writes about symptoms of general lassitude and an inability to concentrate. He says that his early ardour and enthusiasm have mysteriously waned and that things have gone downhill rapidly – his normal capacity for energetic study is diminishing inexplicably:

'I was infinitely happy in this course of life for some months; till at last, about the beginning of September, 1729, all my ardour seemed in a moment to be extinguished, and I could no longer raise my mind to that pitch, which formerly gave me such excessive pleasure.'

This malady of low spirits continued for nine months. Hume goes on to say that he eventually consulted a local physician who diagnosed a 'disease of the learned'. The advice he was given, and to which he submitted, was to take a 'course of bitters and anti-hysteric pills', drink 'an English pint of claret wine every day' and ride 'eight or ten Scotch miles a day'. Hume explains that there was some relief, but this proved only temporary and he found himself unable to concentrate, which was very unusual for him, because he was used to being able to read and write for many hours without losing his focus. This meant that he could not explain ideas properly and his writing became stylistically clumsy. This, for Hume, was the worst part of his malady:

'Here lay my greatest calamity. I had no hopes of delivering my opinions with such elegance and neatness, as to draw to me the attention of the world, and I would rather live and die in obscurity than produce them maimed and imperfect.' (quoted in Grieg, 1932)

Here we see Hume's intense concern for style, a yearning for elegance and precision that he continues to pursue all his life. He finishes the letter with a heartfelt set of questions to the doctor:

'The questions which I would humbly propose to you are: Whether, among all those scholars you have been

acquainted with, you have ever known any affected in this manner? Whether I can ever hope for a recovery? Whether I must long wait for it? Whether my recovery will ever be perfect, and my spirits regain their former spring and vigour, so as to endure the fatigue of deep and abstruse thinking?' (quoted in Grieg, 1932)

Some scholars attribute Hume's depressive illness to a crisis in his religious views (Stewart, 2005) and suggest that he may have been finding it impossible to reconcile the faith of his youth with his later philosophy. There is some evidence for this in James Boswell's recollection of the death of Hume in 1776. Boswell tells us that Hume said he was religious when he was young, and would often test his character against the list of vices in a book called *The Whole Duty of Man* (1658). The list of vices recorded there is fearsomely long and contains amongst them the solemn warning that 'good fellowship' is a waste of time. As we shall see, this warning will be entirely ignored by Hume in later life.

We do not know if Hume lost his faith in God entirely, but he certainly became very sceptical of the claims of traditional Christian belief. The ponderous solemnity and joy-crushing nature of books like *The Whole Duty of Man* – a popular and influential devotional book of the time – may have had something to do with his loss of belief, as well as his eventual philosophical views. We shall see that many of Hume's contemporaries were in no doubt that he was a notorious and dangerous atheist.

Hume's illness appears to have lasted around four or five years (1729–34), and there is no evidence that this kind of malady ever afflicted him again. Indeed, in *My Own Life*, he reports that much of his life had been spent in good spirits despite the occasional disappointments caused by the reception to some of his works. Even as death approached, he said that he had not 'suffered a moment's abatement in my spirits [...] I possess the same ardour as ever in study, and the same gaiety in company'.

Escape to France and the *Treatise*

In 1734, shortly after writing the mysterious letter, Hume 'made a feeble trial for entering into a more active scene of life' (Hume, 1776) and left Scotland, moving to Bristol in the west of England to work as a clerk for a sugar importer. He had vowed to learn about the business world, but within a few months realized that he was ill-suited to the work. However, the break from studying seems to have restored his mental health, and he decided to travel to France, where he says,

> *'I laid that plan of life which I have steadily and successfully pursued. I resolved to make a very rigid frugality to supply my deficiency of fortune, to maintain unimpaired my independency, and to regard every object as contemptible except the improvement of my talents in literature.'* (Hume, 1776)

Hume travelled first to Paris, then on to Rheims (northeast of Paris) for a year, but finding it too expensive, he moved to a small town called La Flèche (west of Paris). La Flèche's principal claim to fame was that its Jesuit monastery had provided the philosopher René Descartes with much of his early education. It was the second most important Jesuit college in France and had a vast library – of around 40,000 books – providing Hume with a

Fig. 2 The Jesuit College of La Flèche where Hume spent time in the vast library.

perfect place to read and write (Gopnik, 2009). He also enjoyed discussing ideas with the Jesuits, and claimed to have hit upon a philosophical argument while 'walking in the cloisters of the Jesuit college of la Flèche [...] engaged in a conversation with a Jesuit of some parts and learning' (quoted in Grieg, 1932). Hume lived in La Flèche for two years, and it was here that he wrote one of the most important works in Modern philosophy: *A Treatise on Human Nature* (1739). After leaving France, he went to stay at his brother's country house in Scotland, where his mother was also residing at the time.

After the publication of the first two volumes of the *Treatise*, Hume seemed to expect the entire philosophical and literary world to hearken enthusiastically to his relentless, sceptical pursuing of what he saw as the pretensions of human reason. They listened, but either misunderstood, or just as enthusiastically rejected his ideas. Hume was desperately disappointed. In *My Own Life*, he tells us that the *Treatise* 'fell dead-born from the press, without reaching such distinction, as even to excite a murmur among the zealots'.

This is a curious exaggeration because the book was widely reviewed. But Hume's disappointment is perhaps explained by his naïve belief that more people would be persuaded by the logic of his argument. In later life, Hume rewrote the first book of the *Treatise* and published the eventual rewrite with some very important additional chapters, one of which is a sceptical attack on the credibility of testimony as to the miraculous.

Hume's disappointment with the *Treatise* is manifest in his avowal that it was delivered, he says, in the 'heat of youth' (quoted in Grieg, 1932) and that it should be entirely ignored. He asked that his new 1748 work – *An Enquiry concerning Human Understanding* – be regarded as his final say on philosophical matters. In other words, he did not want the *Treatise* to represent him as a writer. The language, he feels, was too clumsy and his expressive powers had not yet reached their peak. Generations of scholars have ignored Hume's rejection of his own work, and the *Treatise* is usually taken to be his principal philosophical opus. One wonders what Hume would have thought of this.

Becoming an Essayist

After his disappointment with the *Treatise*, Hume settled on the idea of becoming an essay writer, which was, at the time, as popular as the modern day blog. Writers such as Joseph Addison (1672–1719) and Richard Steele (1672–1729), writing in the immensely successful periodicals *The Spectator* and *The Tatler*, had taken the essay form and reinvented it. This new essay form, published as part of an eagerly awaited periodical, spread like wildfire. One scholar says that 'periodical essays [...] flooded the country and met the eye in every bookseller's shop and coffee-house' (Jack, 1982). Given what he had perceived to be the non-success of the *Treatise*, it is hardly surprising that Hume tried his hand at what could prove to be a real literary winner.

Hume published a collection of essays, *Essays Moral and Political* in 1741–2, and they became a moderate success. He wrote that they 'were favourably received, and soon made me entirely forget my former disappointment' (Hume, 1776). In all probability, Hume learned to write with more clarity by the discipline of these essays, as the 1748 revision of the first book of the *Treatise* is a lot easier to read, and stylistically much more elegant.

Rejection from Academia

In 1745, three years after the publication of his essays, Hume applied for the vacant Chair (professorship) of Moral Philosophy at Edinburgh University, but was rejected. By then, his authorship of the *Treatise* was well-known (though he had published it anonymously), and Hume was accused of 'heresy, deism, scepticism' and, most scandalous of all, 'atheism' (quoted in Grieg, 1932). The charges were named in a short pamphlet entitled *A Specimen of the Principles concerning Religion and Morality, etc.* which is thought to have been written by Reverand William Wishart, the Principal of Edinburgh University, who, along with Frances Hutcheson and William Leechman, was instrumental in blocking Hume's candidacy. Hume reproduced the words from this pamphlet, together with a refutation of its arguments, in 'A Letter from a Gentleman', published on 21 May 1745. It was one of the few times that Hume responded to critics.

The six charges levelled against Hume were as follows: universal scepticism; downright atheism; errors concerning the very being and existence of a God; Errors concerning God's being the First Cause; denying the immateriality of the soul; and 'denying the natural and essential Difference betwixt Right and Wrong' (quoted in Norton & Norton, 2007). Hume argued that his scepticism did not lead him to a position of universal doubt, but merely sought to counteract the idea of absolute certainty that was espoused by other philosophers. He also argued that it was a 'service to piety' to demonstrate the limits of reason when considering the 'great mysteries' of the Christian religion. Careful though he was to use only arguments that had already been put forward by indisputably Christian philosophers, the charges stuck. And as university posts required that their occupants teach a considerable amount of religious instruction, it is perhaps not surprising that Hume was rejected. Even if the charges are false, it is hard to envisage Hume giving any kind of real enthusiasm to his duties to instruct the young in religious affairs.

It is probable that throughout this period in Hume's life he was trying to be financially independent, seeking one position after the next. In 1745 his mother died, and his older brother John inherited the family property and fortune; while as the younger brother, David would have inherited nothing. Consequently, in that same year, and following his rejection from the university, Hume took up the position of tutor to the Marquess of Annadale, which came with a healthy salary of £300 a year (about £48,500 in today's money). The Marquess' household was located in Weld Hall near St Albans, England. The appointment, however, was not a success. The 25-year-old Marquess suffered from depression, had fits of violence and was eventually diagnosed a lunatic. Hume became ensnared in an argument with the Marquess's mother and resigned his position in the spring of 1746.

Joining the Army

After this debacle, Hume was invited to join a military expedition by Lieutenant-General James St Clair, acting as his Secretary. St Clair had been instructed to mount an expedition against French Canada. However, bad weather and indecision on the part of the Admiralty meant the expedition was unexpectedly redirected to the coast of Brittany, France (it was so sudden that St Clair was forced to buy a map of France from a shop in Plymouth before setting sail). Unsurprisingly, the assault failed (but found literary fame in Voltaire's appendix to his *History of the War of 1741* (1756)). This was the last of Hume's military endeavours, but he insisted on wearing the uniform of an officer while joining St Clair on a diplomatic position to Vienna and Turin in 1748 – the same year that the rewrite of the first volume of the Treatise was published with its initial title, *Philosophical Essays Concerning Human Understanding*. (In 1758 it was renamed *An Enquiry Concerning Human Understanding*.)

In 1749 Hume returned to Scotland, where he lived with his brother John and sister Katherine in Ninewells, before moving to Edinburgh in 1751. A little while later he was joined by his sister, and in the same year he published his new book, *An Enquiry Concerning the Principles of Morals*.

Writing History

As if one rejection were not enough, Hume put himself forward again (somewhat reluctantly) for a university post, this time at the University of Glasgow. He was again unsuccessful. It is likely that the unorthodox nature of his views caused the rejection, and Hume himself may have been somewhat relieved.

However, he was successful in another job application, and in 1752 became the Librarian of the Advocates in Edinburgh, a post which gave him access to a large collection of books. Here he was also able to find the time to write a monumental work which was to become his most successful work in terms of popularity. The first volume of *The History of Great Britain*, which was published in 1754, met with a clamour of disapproval. In *My Own Life* Hume says that he was assailed by a unanimous cry of

> 'reproach, disapprobation, and even detestation; English, Scotch, and Irish, Whig and Tory, churchman and sectary, freethinker and religionist, patriot and courtier, united in their rage [...] and after the first ebullitions of their fury were over, what was still more mortifying, the book seemed to sink into oblivion.'

Hume says that he felt so discouraged that 'had not the war been at that time breaking out between France and England, I had certainly retired to some provincial town of the former kingdom, have changed my name, and never more have returned to my native country'. However, noting that this was not possible, and that the second volume of *The History of Great Britain* was already 'considerably advanced', he resolved to 'pick up courage and persevere' (Hume, 1776).

Despite this initial setback, Hume was much more successful with the eventual six volumes of the history, which were published over a period of eight years (1754–62). He was happy to report that once all six volumes had been published, he found that he was 'not only independent, but opulent' (Hume, 1776). The history books became huge best sellers, making more money than ever 'known in England' (Hume, 1776). Indeed, for a long time, Hume was known in the scholarly world as a historian rather than a philosopher. It was not until relatively recently that his philosophy was seen to be much more significant.

Hume was obviously proud of his success. Perhaps part of the reason for this comes from the contemporary publishing situation. In Hume's time, the balance of power between author and publisher was very one-sided in favour of the publisher. Basically, the publisher became to all intents and purposes the employer of the writer. Even the most famous authors either had to publish their writings at their own expense or have a rich patron to help them achieve some degree of independence. Failing that, they would have to obey the dictates of the all-powerful publisher. Hume, however, managed to tip the power balance more towards himself (Harris, 2015). This degree of freedom was indeed unusual and certainly something to be proud of as it meant he could write about whatever he wanted, and in the manner that he thought appropriate.

A Celebrity in Paris

Now aged over 50, Hume decided to settle down in Scotland, determining 'never more to set my foot out of it' (Hume, 1776). But in 1763, he received an invitation to become Secretary to the British Embassy in Paris. He initially refused, thinking that perhaps the 'civilities and gay company of Paris' would disagree with his old, settled, bachelor ways. But, on a second request he agreed to go and found it very different from Britain. He tells us that the more he recoiled from the 'excessive civilities' of the French capital, the more he was lavished with them, resulting

Fig. 3 David Hume, painted by Allan Ramsay in 1766 when Hume was 55 years old.

in a 'real satisfaction in living in Paris'. The city 'abounds' with 'polite company [...] above all places in the universe'. Indeed, he was so struck with the pleasure of being there that he thought of settling in Paris for life (Hume, 1776).

Part of the reason for Hume's love of Paris was the contrast between the life of a 'man of letters' in London, and that of the same kind of man in Paris. London, Hume tells a friend, is stiff, formal and cold: 'The little company there that are worth conversing with are cold and unsociable or are warmed only by faction and cabal.' In Paris, however, there is immediate warmth: 'a man that distinguishes himself in letters, meets immediately with regard and attention' (quoted in Harris, 2015). Hume arrived in Paris and was met, for the first time, with a tremendous amount of attention – those 'excessive civilities' that he wrote about.

Now in his fifties, a contemporary described him at that point as being 'broad and fat, his mouth wide, and without any other expression than that of imbecility' (Harris, 2015). Nonetheless, he was being graced and complimented, wined and dined by the French aristocracy and, to his great surprise, getting plenty of female attention.

Hume found himself the celebrated centre of the Parisian 18th-century scene. In the French Court there was a group of formidable women who dominated the tables and salons of Paris, and it was Hume that they wanted by their side. He was the latest prize and everyone wanted to be seen with him. He was even given a nickname while in Paris: *Le Bon David* (Good Old David). Horace Walpole, the English novelist, wrote, 'It is incredible the homage they pay him' and added that 'Mr Hume is fashion itself' (quoted in Mazza, 2012).

But it was not all plain sailing, however. Hume, at least to begin with, found it all rather overwhelming, with the lavish attention far too excessive. He described it as agreeable 'neither in expectation, possession, nor recollection' and was enjoyable only once the 'circle of [his] acquaintances' had been 'contracted' (quoted in Harris, 2015). Hume was a man who enjoyed the intimacy of a small circle of friends and felt uncomfortable being the (probably awkward) celebrity in the centre of a large crowd.

There was one great attraction of the Parisian scene, however, that Hume did welcome. Comtesse Marie-Charlotte Hippolyte de Boufflers, known as Madame de Boufflers, was one of the 'Great Ladies' of the Paris salons. She had written to Hume in 1761 and, later, attempted to organize a meeting with him in London in early 1763, which never materialized as Hume was out of town. Meeting for the first time at the end of that year in what would be Hume's first winter in Paris, they developed a very close, intense relationship. Hume's correspondence with the Comtesse was extensive and sometimes florid in tone. Scholars are unsure whether the language is indicative of some kind of burgeoning romance or more due to the rich, excessive and zealous language expected in such correspondence. Was it romance or etiquette? It is hard to know. One thing, however, is certain. It was the Comtesse who initiated a train of events that was to have a big impact upon Hume and threatened to ruin his reputation.

The Rousseau Affair

Jean-Jacques Rousseau (1712–78), one of the more controversial philosophers of the Enlightenment, was at that time living in exile having published two controversial texts, one after the other; *The Social Contract* and *Èmile* (1762). Unlike many of his French contemporaries, Rousseau was not an atheist, but he certainly wanted Christianity to be shorn of what he perceived to be its over-reliance upon dogma. The overriding theme in *Èmile* was a rejection of original sin and divine revelation, which was offensive to both Catholic and Protestant beliefs. As a result, his books were banned and burned in both Paris and Geneva, and a warrant was put out for Rousseau's arrest.

The Comtesse suggested to Hume that Rousseau find asylum in England, to which Hume enthusiastically agreed, writing that 'there is no man in Europe of whom I have entertained a higher idea, and whom I would be proud to serve' (quoted in Harris, 2015). Hume offered to use his influence to help Rousseau find a place and a pension in England and so, in early January 1766, at the end of his placement as Secretary to the Embassy in Paris, Hume left for London in the company of Rousseau.

Arriving in London, Hume introduced Rousseau into society and at first all was well. Hume and Rousseau certainly had an affinity with one other: of similar age, neither toed the line and they were both considered controversial for their radical views. However, shortly after his arrival in London, Rousseau – prone to paranoia – began to suspect Hume of being at the centre of a plot to subject him to ridicule. Horace Walpole wrote a mock letter, supposedly from Frederick of Prussia, telling Rousseau that he would be only too happy to subject him to the persecution that Rousseau seemed so intent upon enjoying (Harris, 2015). Rousseau suspected Hume of helping to write the letter, and even went as far as to claim that Hume's generosity was only further evidence of his malicious ingenuity in the conspiracy against him.

Rousseau was one of the greatest writers in Europe at the time. His prose was witty, engaging and intelligent. Despite his notoriety, he wasn't without influence, and the weapon of his prose could likely destroy a reputation. It may be that fear of a character assassination forced Hume to publish an account of the whole affair – perhaps he felt that he must speak first, before Rousseau's pen set out to destroy him. Certainly he was encouraged by some of the French Enlightenment thinkers with whom Rousseau had fallen out. The resulting pamphlet, *A Concise and Genuine Account of the Dispute between Mr Hume and Mr Rousseau* (published in French and English in 1766) is another of the rare times that Hume replied to criticism. It is obvious that Hume did so with some reluctance, writing to the Comtesse that publishing Rousseau's accusatory letters would 'utterly ruin this unhappy man' (quoted in Harris, 2015).

Facing Death

In 1767, Hume took up his last appointment in the Cabinet of the British government as Under-Secretary of State for the Northern Department (which would become the Foreign Office). The following year he retired from public life and in 1769 he returned to Edinburgh, where he built a house for himself in St Andrew's Square in Edinburgh's New Town. In 1771 he and his sister Katherine moved in together.

Hume spent his final years re-reading the classics and keeping up with Scottish writers of politics and history (he considered Scottish writing to be superior to English). He also painstakingly edited his writings, trying to find ever more felicitous and engaging ways of expressing his views so that he might be understood by all.

In 1776, Hume knew that he was very seriously ill, with some (possibly cancerous) 'disorder in [the] bowels'. But writing just before his death, he notes that

> *'I have suffered very little pain from my disorder; and what is more strange, have, notwithstanding the great decline of my person, never suffered a moment's abatement of my spirits; insomuch, that were I to name a period of my life, which I should most choose to pass over again, I might be tempted to point to this later period.'* (Hume, 1776)

He was determined to show the waiting world that he, a notorious sceptic and supposed atheist, could die with courage and equanimity. James Boswell was present when Hume died, on 25 August 1774, and described finding Hume 'placid and even

Fig. 4 Tomb of David Hume, Old Calton Cemetery, Edinburgh.

cheerful [...] talking of different matters with a tranquillity of mind and a clearness of head which few men possess at any time' (quoted in Rasmussen, 2017).

Boswell reported that Hume faced death bravely, despite his lack of religious faith. It seems that some people, who disliked his views, would have preferred him to die in fear and terror. Samuel Johnson (1709–84), for example, when told that Hume had met his end bravely, said that Hume must be a madman (see Harris, 2015). But he did die bravely despite Johnson's expectations. Hume said that he was no more afraid of being dead than he was of his non-existence before he was born.

This kind of detached attitude towards death reveals Hume's preference for classical learning. One of Hume's favourite authors was the philosopher, Epicurus (341–270 BCE), who taught that it is entirely logical that one should be unconcerned with death. He argued that 'where death is, I am not' – death is non-existence and you cannot be harmed when non-existent. The only harms that can come to you are those which happen when you are alive. Death cannot be a harm and should therefore be faced with unconcerned equanimity. It was this attitude that Hume chose to adopt.

In the final paragraph of *My Own Life*, Hume tries to sum up what kind of person he thinks that he is. He deliberately uses the past tense:

'I was, I say, a man of mild dispositions, of command of temper, of an open, social, and cheerful humour, capable of attachment, but little susceptible of enmity, and of great moderation in all my passions. Even my love of literary fame, my ruling passion, never soured my humour, not withstanding my frequent disappointments. My company was not unacceptable to the young and careless, as well as to the studious and literary; and as I took a particular pleasure in the company of modest women, I had no reason to be displeased with the reception I met from them.'

What was Hume like then? We can say this: Hume was a superbly clear and master stylist, a lover of being in a small group of intimate friends, and in such an environment, a gregarious and witty companion, a man of moderate emotions, disliking excessive enthusiasm. He was honest. He was sceptical about the pretensions of reason, but not of ordinary life, and so he sought escape by ordinary habits of being absorbed in work, drinking wine and being in the company of others. His good friend, the economist Adam Smith, said in a eulogy written to their mutual publisher, William Strahan, that his unbelieving friend approached 'as nearly to the idea of a perfectly wise and virtuous man as perhaps the nature of human frailty will permit' (Rasmussen, 2017).

David Hume's Timeline

David Hume	World Events

David Hume

- **1711** April 26th, David Hume born in Edinburgh.
- **1713** Hume's father, Joseph Home, dies.
- **1722** Enrols at Edinburgh University at the age of ten.
- **1725 -29** Begins study to become a lawyer.
- **1729** Falls into a long despression; abandons plans of a career in the law.
- **1734** Leaves Scotland for Bristol before going to France.
- **1734 -37** Writes *A Treatise of Human Nature*
- **1739** Publishes Books I & II of the *Treatise* anonymously.
- **1740** Publishes Book III of the *Treatise*, plus the *Abstract* (to clarify its basic ideas).
- **1741 -42** Publishes *Essays, Moral and Political* anonymously.
- **1745** Applies and is rejected for post of Professor of Moral Philosophy at Edinburgh; Hume's mother dies.
- **1751** Publishes *An Enquiry concerning the Principles of Morals*; writes but does not publish *Dialogues Concerning Natural Religion*.
- **1752** Denied another university post, this time at Glasgow University; publishes *Political Discourses*.

World Events

- **1718** Smallpox inoculation begins in England.
- **1722** Robert Walpole becomes the first Prime Minister of Britain.
- **1726** Publication of Jonathan Swift's *Gulliver's Travels*.
- **1727** George I dies and George II's reign begins; death of Isaac Newton.
- **1733** Publication of Alexander Pope's *Essay on Man*.
- **1735** William Hogarth produces his series of paintings called *A Rake's Progress*
- **1742** British confidence expressed in the writing of the song *Rule Britannia*.
- **1746** Battle of Culloden where the Jacobite army under 'Bonnie Prince Charlie' is defeated.
- **1753** British Museum opens.

1755	Writes essays 'On Suicide' and the 'Immortality of the Soul'.	1755	Lisbon earthquake kills an estimated 100,000 people; publication of Samuel Johnson's *Dictionary of the English Language*.

1755 — Writes essays **'On Suicide'** and the **'Immortality of the Soul'**.

1754 -62 — Publishes the six volumes of **The History of England**, a best seller making Hume independent and very rich.

1763 — Takes on post of Secretary to Embassy in Paris.

1766 — Returns to England with Jean-Jacques Rousseau.

1767 — Becomes Under-secretary of State; expresses sympathy with the American Colonies.

1768 — Retires from public office.

1769 — Returns to Edinburgh.

1770 — Has a house built for himself in Edinburgh New Town.

1772 — Health declines.

1776 — July 4th, Hume invites friends to a farewell dinner; August 25th, Hume dies.

1779 — His nephew, guided by Hume's wishes, publishes **Dialogues Concerning Natural Religion**.

1755 — Lisbon earthquake kills an estimated 100,000 people; publication of Samuel Johnson's **Dictionary of the English Language**.

1759 — Publication of Lawrence Sterne's **Tristram Shandy** and Voltaire's **Candide**.

1763 — Seven Years' War ends with the Treaty of Paris.

1764 — John Harrison's chronometer wins prize for solving the longitude problem.

1768 — James Cook sails to Pacific for the first time aboard **HMS Endeavour**.

1773 — Boston Tea Party – a protest against British taxation.

1774 — Louis XV dies and Louis XVI becomes King of France.

1776 — July 4th, American Declaration of Independence; publication of Adam Smith's **Wealth of Nations**.

2. Influences on Hume's Thinking

As Hume was growing up, a great intellectual war was being waged in Europe. Two fundamentally opposed world views faced each other. One view claimed that humanity was gifted with extraordinary powers of mind. It believed that, by the proper and careful application of reason, it was possible to arrive at sure and certain knowledge of the ultimate nature of reality. Appropriately enough, this view is traditionally called 'rationalism' because it is so confident of the powers of human reason, or rationality. The second view, which came to be known as 'empiricism' claimed that reason is not enough; experience and experiments are also essential for us to reach true knowledge of the world in which we live. These two positions played an important part in creating the background in which Hume evolved as a philosopher.

Rationalism

The typical rationalist philosopher thinks that although experiments and experience are sometimes helpful, they will always play a secondary role to rational deductions made at the desk or sitting in an armchair thinking through the logic of concepts. Philosophers who preceded Hume and took a rationalist position were French philosopher René Descartes (1596–1650), the Dutch philosopher Baruch Spinoza (1632–77) and the German polymath Gottfried Wilhelm Leibniz (1646–1716).

One outstanding example of the intellectual ambition of rationalism and its extraordinary confidence in the power of reason is Leibniz's short work, *The Monadology*. This was written in 1714, when Hume was just three years old, and it is a summary of Leibniz's understanding of reality. It is a very intense and condensed work, and the modern reader is struck – even bewildered – by its exceptional confidence, and by how far Leibniz's ideas are from ordinary lived experience. Leibniz was an extraordinary mathematician, and he believed the whole world could be known with a purity of thought that can be brought to mathematics.

The world we inhabit, said Leibniz, is a divinely created world and it is also the best possible one that God could have chosen. The whole of reality is fundamentally non-physical, being entirely made up of 'mind-like substances' capable of having ideas and perceptions. The physical matter (such as our bodies and other things) that we perceive as moving around are merely phenomena; they are not themselves substances, though they are grounded ultimately in simple substances or monads (single-celled organism), which have collected together.

This collection of minds or monads are related to each other by an incredibly complex array of logical relationships. In addition, each monad mirrors the whole of the rest of the universe. But, Leibniz insists, there are no causal relationships between any of the parts in this infinitely complicated structure. A hammer does not drive the nail into the wood – instead God has made nails whose piercing movements will coincide with the moving of the appropriate hammers. God has set up a pre-established harmony between all the parts of the world so that the nail moves in apparent response to the hammer's blows. *The Monadology* is breathtaking in its confidence. Throughout the work not one murmur of doubt is expressed. Leibniz was possibly the greatest polymath of all time – who wrote papers on the foundations of physics, and was, with Newton, the discoverer of the differential calculus. He was certainly no idle dreamer building philosophical castles in the air. Nevertheless, he presupposed that rationality was deeply embedded in all of nature.

Hume on Rationalism

Hume was aware of rationalist philosophies such as Leibniz's and a central part of his own philosophy is, in effect, a rejection of such boundless metaphysical confidence. He calls such works 'speculative metaphysics' which is a polite way of saying that he thinks they are little more than random guesses. He declares such works to be journeys in 'fairy land' (Hume, 1748). He even says, in a flight of rhetorical excess, that they contain nothing but lies and nonsensical babble and should be burnt:

> *'If we take in our hand any volume; of divinity or school metaphysics, for instance; let us ask, Does it contain any abstract reasoning concerning quantity or number? No. Does it contain any experimental reasoning concerning matters of fact and existence? No. Commit it then to the flames: for it can contain nothing but sophistry and illusion.'* (Hume, 1748)

Hume firmly subscribed to the other world view which was beginning to dominate the intellectual heart of Europe, and would later become known as 'empiricism'. Philosophers (and others) who held this view were very suspicious of the power of unaided human reason. They asked questions such as: are we really as amazing as we think we are? Do we really have God-gifted powers of reason that can lay bare and unlock the secrets of the universe or are we much more fallible than this?

Empiricism

Those with an empiricist philosophy were much less certain that human reason alone could fulfil the tasks that rationalists thought it was able to do. The empiricists agreed that pure reason, bereft of experience, is a poor tool. Doesn't it take experience and experiments, as well as reason, to allow us to investigate reality? We can't do it from the armchair. We have to rise from our desks and go to the laboratory. Philosophers who represent the empiricist camp are the Englishman John Locke (1632–1704), Irish Bishop George Berkeley (1685–1753), and of course, Hume.

Imagine the wide-eyed, 10-year-old Hume beginning his university career. The following quote was the preface to the Logic course, as taught by Colin Drummond, the Professor of Logic and Metaphysics and dictated to his students during the study year of 1722–23. It is probable that they were the first words of philosophy that the young Hume would hear at an inaugural address given to new students:

> 'The human mind is endowed by its creator with such
> extensive faculties that, if it would use the same aright,
> it could both know and delight in God himself [...]

[The human mind] has very many gifts vouchsafed to it, natural and supernatural alike, by which it may recognize its duty and learn to persist in a right course [...] Philosophy is the certain and evident knowledge of matters both divine and human that can be procured by a human being through the light of nature.' (Quoted in Stewart, 2005)

These words give a good indication of the prevailing presuppositions of much of the culture and thought of the day. As can be seen, the words overflow with rationalist confidence in our mental powers. Through the divinely bestowed 'light of reason' we can have 'sure and evident knowledge'.

Rejecting the Image of God in Man

Why exactly were the rationalists so confident in the powers of human reasoning? There are many answers. Part of the reason is the impressive way that certainty can be attained in the purely rational activities of geometry and mathematics (many of the rationalists were brilliant mathematicians) – but its most important foundation is the Judeo-Christian belief that humans are made in the image and likeness of God. This doctrine is often referred to by its Latin name, *imago Dei* (the image of God). It derived from the Bible's opening chapters of Genesis, and was immensely influential.

The rationalists believed that the way in which we imitate or mirror God is in our rational faculties. Our minds, they said, are finite imitators of the omniscient mind of God. (Leibniz went as far as to say that each mind reflects the whole of the rest of reality from its own point of view and so is, in a sense, actually omniscient!) This view obviously raised a few difficult questions, forcing Descartes to devote a whole chapter of his *Meditations* (1641) to an explanation on how it is possible for humans to make mistakes. If God gave us our faculties and God is not a deceiver, how is it even possible for us to make any errors? (It is not clear that Descartes managed to find a good answer to this question.)

The rationalists would be ready to admit that our minds are finite and impoverished due to the effects of sin, but nevertheless they believed that the divine fire of rationality continues to burn very brightly within us. Just like God, we can have certainty merely by thinking through the logic of ideas. God, of course, does not have to conduct experiments to find out what will happen – and in so far as we are like the divine, neither do we. Furthermore, we can come to an infallible certainty that we are right. In this way, part of the rationalists' confidence derived from a religious source. In their view, we are beings with a kind of divine status whose minds can illuminate the very fabric and structure of the universe just by thinking about it in the right way.

The Experimental Method

The battle that took place between rationalism and empiricism during the Enlightenment (which we will say more of in due course) resulted in empiricism winning the hearts and minds of Europe. One important publication which is considered a helping factor is the 1687 publication of *Mathematical Principles of Natural Philosophy* by Isaac Newton (1642–1727), probably the greatest physicist-mathematician of all time. In this great work Newton investigated the laws of motion, the tides, the laws of gravitation, and laid the entire groundwork for classical mechanics.

Newton's methods were firmly experimental. He conducted experiments with prisms. He looked at tide tables. He investigated what spheres do when they roll down inclined planes. He timed the swings of pendulums. In other words, he nourished his intellect with lavish amounts of experience. Like most of his fellow experimentalists and empiricists, he was sceptical about the power of human reason. This was not because he refused to believe that we are mirrors of God – Newton was an ardent, though unorthodox believer. His scepticism about the power of reason was due to theological ideas about the way sin has ruined our cognitive capacities. One of his most famous utterances is the declaration 'I feign no hypotheses' ('*Hypotheses non fingo*'); which basically means that his physics set out to describe and predict what happens without necessarily trying to explain it.

Even when he spoke about gravity, Newton was stunningly hesitant about what exactly he had discovered. What exactly is gravity? he asks. He replied that he had no idea at all. How can gravity affect something else at a distance? Newton said that such a notion veers towards absurdity:

> '*That gravity should be innate, inherent, and essential to matter, so that one body may act upon another at distance through a vacuum, without the mediation of anything else [...] is to me so great an absurdity that I believe no man who has in philosophical matters a competent faculty of thinking can ever fall into it.*'
> (quoted in Urmson, 1982)

Newton was a firm believer in the prevailing scientific methodology, which always tried to explain natural phenomena in mechanical terms. This means that all phenomena should be explicable in terms of contact between bodies and their movements and shapes. The clock is the paradigm mechanical device: cogs turn other cogs due to the influence of their shape and their contact with each other. The idea that there might be forces of attraction and repulsion without contact was seen as bordering on the occult or mystical rather than normal science. For the mechanical philosophy, our understanding of reality such as it is must be traceable to some concrete, actual experience, not some invisible force between objects.

Newton's thought and this 'experimental method' (which was renamed 'empiricism' in the 19th century) was incredibly influential. And, as we know, it was an immense success – there was a rapid expansion of knowledge gained through empirical science. Things really did seem to work according to the laws laid down by Newton, which had used reason to reflect upon the results of experiential tests. The data collected through testing and experimenting in the physical world was a vital part of his discoveries, and of scientific discoveries ever since. It is also a rejection of the primacy of unaided reason. From this point on, people gained a greater scepticism about their ability to see into the heart of things using their minds alone.

Hume the Empiricist

Hume was profoundly influenced by these ideas, and their accompanying empiricist methodology. He saw himself as trying to emulate experimental methodology in what he calls the 'moral sciences' (what we would call the human sciences – the word 'moral' had a much wider meaning then than it has today).

We can see this in the subtitle to his first philosophical work, *A Treatise of Human Nature*. The subtitle says the work is 'an attempt to introduce the experimental method of reasoning into moral subjects [i.e. human subjects]'. Throughout the introduction he uses language that would typically be used by experimenters, and although he does not mention Newton by name, it is obvious that the scientist is a strong influence.

Like Newton and the major experimenters, Hume wanted to be a great empirical investigator – not of prisms and tides, but of the mind itself. He wanted to undertake a careful examination of the nature of our experience, so that he could describe how the human mind works. Hume's constant maxim, in one form or another, is this: say nothing that experience cannot justify. Instead of relying on pure logic and reasoning (which, as we have seen, just lands us in a fairy land of speculation) we must look closely at the nature of our experiences. We must not go beyond experience. Once we do that we are in danger of using words without any understanding of what we are saying. Put another way, we lose meaning and we lose contact with reality. We shall be examining this further when we look at the Copy Principle in Chapter 3.

Enlightenment and Empiricism

Scholars agree that Hume is the most important contributor to the Scottish Enlightenment (and many consider him to be the greatest British philosopher of all time). Hume's philosophy must be seen in the context of the new kind of thinking that evolved in Europe during the 18th century. The centre of the international movement known as the Enlightenment is usually taken to be France, and its culmination is often understood to be the bloody French Revolution of 1789. Here we have such figures as the political philosophers Montesquieu (1689–1755), Voltaire (1694–1778) and Denis Diderot (1713–84).

The Enlightenment is often understood primarily as a cultural and literary phenomenon, where a new set of political, judicial and cultural values were championed. These centred upon a celebration of independent thought and liberty of conscience, a rejection of any meek acceptance of authority (especially religion) combined with a commitment to tolerance of different religions and viewpoints.

But alongside these, there was a scientific and empiricist aspect. Just like Hume, the French Enlightenment thinkers rejected the grand metaphysical theorizing of figures such as Leibniz and Descartes. Empiricist ideals of investigation using the senses and experience were now seen as the way towards any kind of truth, given the fallible nature of the human mind. Many of the heroes of the French Enlightenment thinkers were the pioneers of the empirical method such as Newton and Francis Bacon (1561–1626) whose work *Novum Organon* (1620) laid the basis for the experimental method. 'Novum Organon' means 'New Tool' – and in this work Bacon aimed to replace the 'scientific method' laid out in the Ancient Greek philosopher Aristotle's original *Organon*. Aristotle's philosophical treatise suggested that logical reasoning could be used as a tool for approaching the world, nature and science. It was this that Bacon aimed to replace with a new tool – the scientific method – a process that uses inductive principles and empirical data gathered through observation to find precise answers to natural and scientific phenomena.

In both Bacon and Newton we see a much more modest self-understanding of the rational powers of the mind. Although the Enlightenment is often called the Age of Reason, the 'reason' referred to is not the God-given, semi-divine faculty of the rationalists. Rather, reason's bedrock is experience. What reason allows us to do is order, examine and calculate using the raw materials gathered through our senses. Enlightenment thinkers hoped that if people used reason properly in the service of experience, they would be able to make useful discoveries and find answers to the very down-to-earth problems of humanity.

In other words, speculation about hidden truths should be replaced by clear statements which can be traced back to experiment. This gathering of factual evidence, the empiricists claimed, is more reliable than conclusions drawn by theorizing alone. They saw reason as the servant of experience, not the master, and they saw this as appropriate because reason always finds itself obedient to the urges of experience and human nature.

Hume was profoundly influenced by such ideas. At the age of 18 he complained in a letter (quoted in Grieg, 1932) that philosophy is engaged in 'endless disputes' because it is always based upon theories that are 'entirely hypothetical' and depend 'more upon Invention than Experience'.

He says again and again in his work that reason plays less of a role than we might think it does. Human nature is not centred on the so-called rational – instead it is obedient to the commands of experience. To make progress, Hume maintains, we need to 'reject every system [...] however subtle or ingenious, which is not founded on fact and observation' (Hume, 1748).

Philosophical Influences

We have seen in the intellectual background of Hume's day that there was a slow replacement of one world view with another; a movement towards a new way of perceiving the human mind and its place in nature. In this section we shall get a little more specific and direct, and briefly explore some of the writers who had an influence on Hume.

In the Introduction to *A Treatise on Human Nature* Hume says that we must approach science in a new way. This is a much broader statement than it first appears to be, because in those days the word 'science' meant any field of human knowledge. Hume mentions, for example, religion, politics and morals as well as maths, and 'natural philosophy' (which we now know as 'science'). Hume said that instead of looking outward at the world and attempting to glean knowledge directly from there, we must first turn our eye inwards and inspect ourselves and our own minds. He says:

> 'Here then is the only expedient, from which we can hope for success in our philosophical researches, to leave the tedious lingering method, which we have hitherto followed, and instead of taking now and then a castle or village on the frontier, to march up directly to the capital or centre of these sciences, to human nature itself; which being once masters of, we may everywhere else hope for an easy victory. From this station we may extend our conquests over all those sciences, which more intimately concern human life, and may afterwards proceed at leisure to discover more fully those which are the objects

of pure curiosity [...] We in effect propose a complete system of the sciences, built on a foundation almost entirely new.' (Hume, 1739)

Hume acknowledges that others have tried to put this revised science of man on a new footing, and mentions 'Mr Locke, my Lord Shaftesbury, Dr Mandeville, Mr Hutcheson, Dr Butler, &c.' Other writers who influenced Hume greatly were Dutch philosopher Bernard Mandeville (1670–1733), Anthony Ashley Cooper (1671–1713) the English philosopher and Third Earl of Shaftesbury, known as 'Shaftesbury', and the French philosopher Nicolas Malebranche (1638–1715). Their influences are explored below.

Shaftesbury and Mandeville

In 1711, Shaftesbury published a very influential, three-volume book called *Characteristics of Men, Manners, Opinions, Times.* One of his main contentions was that people are capable of genuine goodness. This was directly oppositional to the view put forward by the brilliant English philosopher Thomas Hobbes (1588–1679), who had argued that all morality is based upon self interest, and that we only do things because we get something out of it. Shaftesbury argued that this was wrong; we are capable of genuine benevolence, he said. Humans are naturally virtuous or good. This optimistic understanding of human nature was not shared by Mandeville.

Bernard Mandeville had emigrated to England once he'd left university in Rotterdam, Holland, and he permanently settled there. His most influential work was the hugely popular *The Fable of the Bees* (1714), in which he sets out to find the principal motivations that people have and how our deepest impulses might work together for the benefit of society. He specifically targets Shaftesbury in this work. Mandeville says that we are not the benevolently rational creatures that we think we are. We are greedy, and more prompted by impulse than reason. He says, 'I believe man (beside skin, flesh, bones, etc. that are obvious to the eye) to be a compound of various passions, that all of them as they are provoked and come uppermost, govern him by turns, whether he will or no' (Mandeville, 1714). In other words, we do things purely out of self-interest. Paradoxically, however, Mandeville argues that our private vices add up to a society that can thrive. This was an idea that was picked up by the Scottish philosopher and economist Adam Smith (1723–90), who argued that a collection of perfectly rational self-interested people will lead to a free-market economy that benefits everyone (an idea still much under discussion).

In the most general terms, we can say that Hume saw in Mandeville an ally who recognized that reason is much less important than we might think it is. We are, indeed, more creatures of habit and impulse ('passions') than calm, rational reflection. This denigration of a certain view of reason is, as we have seen, part of the Enlightenment picture of humankind. Hume also agreed with Mandeville in his rejection of the view that humans have a kind of God-given end to which they are directed. But Hume did not agree with Mandeville that we are incapable of genuine disinterested feelings for others. Here he finds more agreement with Shaftesbury's less pessimistic view of human nature.

Feelings and Morality

Hume argued that an entirely natural reaction to the plight of others is to have sympathy. If we see someone drowning in the river we lose the sense of ourselves and get taken up by their distress; we feel the other's pain as a kind of mental infection. Their distress overcomes us and consequently we forget about ourselves. We do not have to imagine ourselves drowning and then feel how awful that would be to us – that would be Mandeville's analysis, and so, in his understanding, we would be prompted to save the other person because of how awful we feel. Any kind of charitable giving, for Mandeville, is only a way in which we give to some substitute of ourselves. It is all greed. Hume, however, is not so gloomy about our motives. In Hume's way of seeing this situation, we 'tune into' the plight of others, rather than become distressed by our imagining of how it would feel for us to drown.

One very important way, however, in which Hume agrees with Mandeville, Shaftesbury and Hobbes is their separation of morality from religion. They all thought that morality, whatever its actual origins (and here they disagree), can exist without religion. This naturalistic (rather than super-naturalistic, godly given) view of morality is part of Hume's naturalism, which we will discuss below.

Malebranche and Causality

The French priest and philosopher Nicolas Malebranche is mentioned by Hume four times in the *Enquiry on Human Understanding*, and in a letter to a friend (Michael Ramsey, in 1737) Hume says that essential preparatory reading of the

Treatise should include Malebranche's *The Search After Truth* (1674). Malebranche's views had a big impact upon Hume because they alerted him to a problem deep in our conception of causation – which was to become one of Hume's main areas of study. Malebranche argued that our idea of cause and effect is radically mistaken. We suppose that when a ball hits a window there is some kind of energy transference, and that consequently the window breaks because the ball has a certain window-breaking power. This is all wrong, says Malebranche. Balls, mere hunks of matter, cannot have the power that they are supposed to have. It does not make sense. Hume completely agrees with Malebranche's main contention here, but as we shall see in Chapter 3, he completely disagrees with his solution.

Another writer that Hume mentions in his letter to Michael Ramsey is the French writer Pierre Bayle (1647–1706) who wrote the extremely influential *Critical and Historical Dictionary* (publication began in 1697). This is a massive, wide-ranging work of over six million words. Probably one of the principal ways in which Bayle had an influence upon Hume was his all-pervading scepticism. Hume is often credited with being a sceptic in the Baylesian tradition.

Scepticism and Ordinary Life

In his time, Hume was known as being a radical and dangerous sceptic (the Encyclopedia Britannica of 1815–1817 stated that his writings aimed 'to produce in the reader a complete distrust in his own faculties'). This became Hume's reputation. He was seen as dangerous to morality, religion and civil life – an enemy of the established order. There is no doubt that Hume was sceptical. We have seen this in his agreement that the human mind, bereft of experience, is far less capable than the rationalists believed, and inevitably impoverished.

Hume did not always find his scepticism comfortable. In one vivid and memorable passage from the end of Book One of the *Treatise*, he declares himself almost reduced to despair by his philosophical conclusions concerning the fallible ways of the mind. He finds nothing within himself but 'doubt and ignorance'. He is 'utterly abandoned and disconsolate'. We are led by our minds into 'errors, absurdities and obscurities'. Hume had discovered, to his horror, that reason is not the divine gift that the inaugural speech at Edinburgh University had promised. Instead it is based upon the brute force of habit and custom. We are brow-beaten into submission by repetition – hardly the picture of the noble human thinker that many would have held at the time.

How are we to find our way out of the depressing mess that philosophical thinking has led us into? Hume's answer in the *Treatise* is clear. It is ordinary life – those ordinary pursuits that life provides for us if we are lucky enough. Hume says when he is in the 'deepest darkness', the way out is not by thinking about it further, it is by escaping. Ordinary life can cure him of his 'philosophical melancholy and delirium'. How did he intend to do this?

> *'I dine, I play backgammon, I converse, and am merry with my friends, and when after three of four hour's amusement, I wou'd return to speculations, they appear so cold, and strain'd, and ridiculous, that I cannot find in my heart to enter into them any further.'* (Hume, 1739)

Hume eventually came to realize that philosophy leaves the mind untouched at its deepest level. Ordinary life insists upon its reality. Our passions are left undiminished in their power over us despite all our philosophical theorizing.

So it is true that Hume is a great sceptic, but this does not mean, he said, that we leave everything behind and sink into a profound sceptical silence and doubt. It is certainly true that reason is in need of a tremendous amount of humbling. It is far less important than we think it is. After many difficult, and more often than not, sceptical arguments, Hume concludes that reason-induced scepticism makes little practical difference. Human nature always has its way.

Some commentators have pointed out that his scepticism can be understood slightly differently. They say that he could be interpreted as saying that we have misunderstood what it is for something to be 'rational'. We have modelled rationality on the kind of proofs and procedures that are used in mathematics, and then mistakenly applied this impossible standard to other areas of life. We have sought proof, for example, that there really is an external world. But rationality is broader than the mathematical model. On this broader, more generous, interpretation of rationality, it is rational to believe in things which are incapable of being proved.

Hume argues, for example, that we have no rational reason to believe that objects will fall to the earth when dropped, but we cannot help believing that they will. This explains why, when we leave a room, we leave by the door rather than from the window. We cannot help but believe that if we leave the room by the window we shall plummet to the ground. The stairs are the better option, not because it is rational to believe this, but because we have no choice but to believe it.

Ordinary life is our great comfort as we are threatened by the despair of scepticism. No matter what scepticism says, we stubbornly and inevitably cling to the belief that things will fall when they are unsupported. We simply cannot help it. Hume believes that this stubbornness of belief and its obedience to custom and habit is one of the most important facts about human psychology that he discovered using the experimental method.

Naturalism

Hume's approach is often referred to as naturalistic. The triumph of naturalism is another legacy of the Enlightenment that Hume is willing to embrace. Naturalism is difficult to define clearly – it is as much an attitude of mind as it is a philosophical movement. It is partly an attempt to describe, as honestly as possible and without any preconceptions of prejudices, the actual natural facts as they present themselves to experience. Before the advent of naturalism, philosophers were more inclined to describe what they thought ought to be the case rather than to express what is the case. The naturalistic philosopher looks at the way things are as honestly and as directly as possible.

Naturalism also implies a non-religious outlook. The typical naturalistic philosopher, like Hume, does not employ any theological or supernatural accounts to explain the facts. Although Hume refers to God in many parts of his works, he never seems to use God as part of any serious explanation. As a result, scholars are not sure whether Hume was an atheist or not. Are the references to God merely ways in which he can make his writings more acceptable to the prominently religious audiences of the time or did he have some vague belief in a kind of distant divine being? Was he an atheist, or merely a sceptic? Whatever his beliefs, his works consistently strive to discredit the doctrines and dogmas of all types of religious belief.

In 1757, he published *The Natural History of Religion*, in which he tried to explain the causes and origins of religious thought. Religion has thrived, he claims, for a variety of completely natural, psychological reasons. People, he says, are naturally prone to anthropomorphizing – 'we see faces in the moon, armies in the clouds' (Hume, 1757c). This is because 'there is a universal tendency among mankind to conceive all beings like themselves and to transfer to every object, those qualities with which they are familiarly acquainted' (Hume, 1757c). When things go disastrously awry – such as the occurrence of a flood or an earthquake – our natural fear and our natural anthropomorphizing tendencies impel us to see the event as caused by an invisible and powerful person. Terrified, we implore this invisible 'god' to prevent the flood or to stop the earthquake. Hume says that this primitive, natural reaction to events eventually evolves into the monotheistic religions we see today. Religion is explained wholly naturalistically, rather than being seen as the revelations of a supernatural being called God.

It is the same with his investigations of human psychology. Hume attempts to describe all that happens in the human mind in terms of the natural facts and laws of human psychology. Our minds, he claims to discover, are not divinely inspired instruments of magical insight – they obey custom and habit, both of which are just aspects of experience. Indeed, he claims that:

> *'all probable reasoning is nothing but a species of sensation. 'Tis not solely in poetry and music, we must follow our taste and sentiment, but likewise in philosophy [...] When I give preference to one set of arguments above another, I do nothing but decide from my feeling concerning the superiority of their influence.'*
> (Hume, 1739)

This is a remarkable thing to say. If we are convinced by Hume's arguments it is not because we are reasoned into the truth, it is more that what he says resonates with us – 'strikes a chord' we might say.

We also see naturalism at work in Hume's theory of morality. In Hume's time there were many philosophers who thought that unless there is a God, there can be no proper foundation for morality. They argued that we need God as a kind of support. But as we have seen with Hobbes, Shaftesbury and Mandeville, other views were beginning to make themselves more popular.

3. Causation and Induction

Hume's influence on philosophical discussions of cause and effect is probably his greatest philosophical legacy. He discovered a whole host of problems right at the core of our notions of causation – problems which philosophers wrestle with to this day.

In order to understand Hume's radical views about causation, we need to examine what we ordinarily mean when we say that A caused B – when some thing or event causes something else to happen. Let us take Hume's own example. A billiard ball is racing across the table. It strikes another, and this second ball begins to move. We would not think of this as a coincidence, but that the two events were related. We would naturally say that the first ball caused the movement of the second ball.

This relation of causation can be expressed in slightly different ways, but they all seem to mean more or less the same thing. For example, we might say that the first ball made the second ball move; that the first ball gave the second ball the energy or power of motion. We could say that, given the first ball's motion and the laws of nature, the second ball had to move. There is, we think, some kind of energy transfer which enlivens the second ball and forces it to move. To sum up, we think that there is some necessitating connection between the two events which makes the second ball move when it is struck by the first.

Here, then, is the first thing we must note in our ordinary understanding of causation. We think of it as some kind of natural inevitability or necessity. When we see a window being struck by a stone and the window breaking, we do not think that this was a coincidence as if the first event had nothing to do with the second. There is something about the stone's properties and the window's properties that caused/made it the case that the window broke.

There is another important aspect to our understanding of causation which should be made clear. We think that causes and effects and the necessary connections between them exist as extra-mental facts (i.e. facts about the world itself, not within the mind). To talk of Event A causing Event B is to talk about connections between events in the world. It is not just 'in our heads'. Talk of cause and effect is not like talk about our personal tastes. When a person says 'Chocolate is nice' this is essentially about the person and their subjective opinion. There is no property of 'niceness' which somehow inhabits the chocolate. The niceness of the chocolate is in the eye or, in this case, the taste buds of the beholder. We do not think that causes and their effects are like that. Instead we think that causes and effects are independent of us.

Let us look at an example to show what is meant. We think that causation was happening well before human beings were on the scene. If an enormous asteroid hit earth millions of years ago before any sentient life was around, we naturally assume that there would have been certain inevitable effects on the planet

– a lot of destruction for example. These effects would have been caused to happen due to the destructive power and enormous energy of the asteroid. If we think that causes and effects can happen without human observers then we are committed to the idea that causes and effects are there independently of us. They are outside the mind. They are extra-mental facts. To sum up, when we think about causation, we generally agree that:

1. There are necessary connections between things and events.

2. Causes and effects are really 'out there' in the world. Certain objects or events objectively have the power to make other things happen.

Hume said that we have no proper ground to assume either of these two ideas. We cannot legitimately talk about necessary connections between events, neither can we suppose they are really 'out there' in the world. All we can really say, he argues, is that we have grown to expect windows to break when stones hit them. In other words, we have grown a habit of mind or thinking that makes us expect that the one will happen after the other happens. This habit grows more and more entrenched as we are repeatedly exposed to one type of event following another type of event.

For example, when we first saw a billiard ball hitting another, we would have had no expectations. No habits of mind had yet grown. But as we see repeated occasions of billiard ball hitting billiard ball, we grow so accustomed to seeing the movement of the second ball that we now expect that it will move. This is not the result of rational insight or because we see some kind of external necessity – it is merely a habit of mind, a custom of thought acquired in non-rational, conditioned fashion.

This is, indeed, a profoundly sceptical conclusion. Let us reconsider the asteroid hitting earth before any sentient life was around. If causation is in the mind of the beholder, then, there might have been one event following another – an asteroid hitting and after that a lot of destruction, but the one could not have caused or made the other happen since there would be no minds to foist this understanding upon the events. Just as the 'niceness' of chocolate would not exist were there no people to experience it, so there would be no causation.

The Copy Principle

How does Hume arrive at this radical conclusion? In order to explain that, we must examine one of the central planks of his empiricist philosophy, known as the Copy Principle. Hume says,

> *'It seems a proposition, which will not admit of much dispute, that all our ideas are copies of our impressions, or that, in other words, that it is impossible for us to think of anything, which we have not antecedently felt, either in our external or internal senses.'* (Hume, 1748)

Later, in the same book (*An Enquiry Concerning Human Understanding*) he repeats the Copy Principle in similar words: 'Every idea is copied from some preceding impression or sentiment; and where we cannot find an impression, we may be certain that there is no idea.' All our ideas, he says – anything we can think meaningfully about – must have its origin in some prior impression.

By an 'impression' Hume basically means that we have to have some sensory input – some incoming data from experience that makes an impression on our minds, much as an embossing tool upon paper – in order to know what we are talking about. We need, for example, to see blue in order to understand what the word 'blue' means. We have to taste wine to understand what people are talking about when they describe the hints of blackcurrant and cherry that they can taste. Without this initial imprint from the arena of experience, an idea is empty and meaningless. We would be using words as sounds, rather than as content-full expressions.

Here, of course, we witness Hume's firm conviction that experience is the all-powerful force in the foundation of our thoughts. Unless there is a founding experience, our words talk of nothing that we can actually think about. They become mere air.

Meaningless Concepts

The trouble is that the ideas of 'power, force, energy or necessary connection' (Hume, 1748) do not seem to have any initial input from the court of experience. Consequently there is the real threat that the words are mere air – meaningless sounds thrown around with the illusion of understanding.

This is a very serious threat to our ideas about causation. In order to avoid the spectre of meaninglessness, Hume looks for an initiating impression that could be the experiential foundation of meaning for words such as power, force, and necessary connection. His first strategy is to look more carefully at a typical case of where we claim one thing caused another. Perhaps, by a careful and minute examination of a particular event, we might be able to discern an impression of the necessitating connection. (Here, of course, we see Hume's experimental method in action.)

Unfortunately, Hume finds that all we see is one event happening, say, a billiard ball moving and contacting the other, and then the second ball moving. One thing happens, and then another thing happens. That's all. We do not experience the all-important impression of the necessity of its movement. Hume tells us that, no matter how fastidious we are with our scrutiny of a particular causal event, we cannot find the impression of necessity:

> *'We are never able, in a single instance, to discover any power or necessary connexion; any quality, which binds the effect to the cause, and renders the one an infallible consequence of the other. We only find, that the one does actually, in fact, follow the other.'* (Hume, 1748)

Hume strengthens his argument by pointing out that if we have no previous experience of any pair of events, we could not discover by reason alone that the one event would result in the second. But surely, he says, if the effect is an infallible and inevitable consequence of the cause, we should be able to see it. We would, by rational insight, 'see' the causal connection and be able to deduce the inevitable outcome. But we cannot.

Causation relies on the court of experience alone, but there does not seem to be anything in that court that provides what we think we see – the necessitating connection. A careful examination of experience shows us that what we think we see is actually not there. Hume's conclusion is that when we look at events like the motion and striking of billiard balls we do not have any impression that provides meaning for the notion of the necessitating connection. Is there another way in which we might experience the all-important necessary connection?

Internal Control

Perhaps, Hume says, we are looking in the wrong place. Perhaps if we shift our attention from the external world to the internal region of our own thoughts and bodies we might find the beginning of meaning for natural necessity:

> *'It may be said, that we are every moment conscious of internal power; while we feel, that, by a simple command of the will, we can move the organs of our body, or direct the faculties of our mind.'* (Hume, 1748)

For example, if you decide to move your arm, your arm moves. If you wish to think about Paris or think about Rome, you find yourself doing so. Surely here we can see the 'act of volition' making the arm move or bringing Paris or Rome to mind. In other words, we can 'see' by internal observation, the necessitating connection. Is this the experiential foundation for words like 'force', 'power', 'necessary connection' and the like?

Hume's answer is that this cannot be the foundation. He says that our control of our own bodies is a mystery to us and cannot provide the necessary light that might illuminate the necessitating connection. We are in the dark about how our minds work upon the material body. He says, '…is there any principle in all nature more mysterious that the union of soul [i.e. mind] with body […] [how] the most refined thought is able to actuate the grossest matter' (Hume, 1748). Moreover, why is it that we cannot influence all the organs of the body with the same efficacy? I can move my arm, but why can't I, just by a direct act of volition, influence my pancreas? 'This question,' says Hume, 'would never embarrass us, were we conscious of the power' that we are attempting to find (Hume, 1748).

It is similar with the way we are able to direct our own thoughts. We have not the slightest idea how we do it. How is it, that by a mere act of will, we are able to produce a thought as if out of nothing? One minute I am thinking about nothing in particular – the next moment I am able to populate my mind with a multitude of thoughts and images. How am I able to do that? We simply do not know.

Again, why is it that we cannot direct or control our thoughts sometimes? Why is it that thoughts will arise spontaneously? Why is it that I cannot make a thought go away? Hume says, 'Will anyone pretend to assign the ultimate reason of these boundaries […]?' (Hume, 1748). He is confident that no one will be able to reply.

There appears to be nothing in experience to act as a foundation for words to do with causation. A word such as 'table' is based on our experience of a certain type of object – but what in experience could act as the foundation for the word 'causation'? We see that an examination of experience reveals the hollowness behind the rationalist assurance that reason can get to the heart of reality. Our minds simply do not discern things like necessitating connections.

Could it be God?

There was another answer to the problem of causation that was popular in Hume's day. Occasionalists such as Nicolas

Malebranche, who we briefly mentioned in Chapter 2, believed that the connection between thoughts and bodily movement only occurred because of the continuing intervention of God. Occasionalists placed God as 'the necessitator' in nature, saying that God provides the necessitating impetus which makes *all effects* happen. On every occasion of one thing causing another, God is the actuating agent (hence the name 'occasionalist'). In this view, physical matter is seen as mere shape or extension, an idea that originally stemmed from the philosopher René Descartes. Matter's defining property, from this perspective, is its dimensionality – matter is merely the kind of thing which fills a particular portion of space. As such it is simply not the kind of thing that can have any effect on anything else. Matter is considered as passive chunks of stuff.

The essential thought behind Malebranche's proposal is that any causation worth the name must be necessary – the kind of necessity that Hume is looking for. In other words, if A is a cause of B, then, if A happens it is absolutely impossible for B not to happen. The second event comes out of the first as if it were a logical inevitability or the result of a piece of arithmetic, such as 2 + 2 = 4. But Malebranche, like Hume, recognized that causation does not seem to be like this. Mere matter cannot force another event to happen – it is far too weak and passive. For Malebranche, the way out of the impotence of matter was the omnipotence of God. Only God, he said, is powerful enough to enforce the kind of necessity we require of causation. God, therefore, is the strong link, the universal necessitator.

Hume's Three Objections

Hume considers Malebranche's proposal and rejects it. First he explains the nature of the proposal put forward by the Occasionalists like this: 'Instead of saying that one billiard ball moves another by a force which it has derived from the author of nature [i.e. God]; it is the Deity himself, they say, who, by a particular volition, moves the second ball, being determined to this operation by the impulse of the first ball.' (Hume, 1748) Hume goes on to say that it is the 'same ignorance' that leads people to 'assert that the Deity is the immediate cause of the union between soul and body' and also that 'it is not any energy in the will, that produces local motion in our members [limbs]'. God is forced, in this scenario, to 'second our will, in itself impotent'.

Hume's criticism, in *An Enquiry Concerning Human Understanding*, is in three parts. He first says that such a theory diminishes, rather than magnifies, the grandeur of God's attributes. 'It argues surely more power in the Deity to delegate a certain degree of power to inferior creatures, than to produce everything by his own immediate volition', says Hume. And of God's wisdom, he asks, surely it requires more wisdom 'to contrive at first the fabric of the world with such perfect foresight' that it will easily run itself, without intervention?

Hume then suggests turning away from talking about the attributes of a Deity (who may or may not exist, though Hume does not go so far as to say this) and consider the argument from a purely philosophical view.

He moves to his second objection, which is that the occasionalist theory carries no 'conviction'. We are in 'fairy land' he says – a perhaps entertaining place but one that prompts no belief. Try to believe as a real conviction that when you move your arm, God is the one moving it in response to your will. Hume thinks you won't be able to do it. We are in a land of very far-fetched fiction.

His third objection is that putting God into the picture as the link between events is to deepen the mystery of causation not solve it. 'We are ignorant', says Hume, '[…] of the manner in which bodies operate on each other: their force or energy is entirely incomprehensible'. But what incomprehensibility is removed by putting God into the equation? This is to introduce the most mysterious being of all – one whose incomprehensibility is of the highest and deepest order. No, concludes Hume, we cannot get to the necessity that we think is there by introducing God. It is a false solution to the problem.

Is Causation a Meaningless Idea?

We seem to have a big problem. Hume has shown that we gain no impression of necessity from looking at the outside world (e.g., of billiard balls) or from the inner world of thoughts and mental actions. Neither can the introduction of God help. Nevertheless, we do use the word 'necessity'. We do use words like 'energy', 'force', 'power' and the like. But if these are really meaningless sounds, why do they appear to be so full of content? It certainly does not look like nonsense to say that one event necessitated another. It does not appear to be equivalent to some nonsensical statement like 'one event jabberwocked another'. So where then does the appearance of content and meaning come from?

Hume tells us that there is still one way that we can avoid reaching the conclusion that the idea of necessity is completely empty of content and meaning. The connection between events is one that we feel as we are exposed to repetitions of the same twin events. We cannot help but expect the second event when the first has occurred. Hume says,

> *'after a repetition of similar instances, the mind is carried by habit, upon the appearance of one event, to expect its usual attendant, and to believe that it will exist. This connexion, therefore, which we feel in the mind, this customary transition of the imagination from one object to its usual attendant, is the sentiment or impression from which we form the idea of necessary power or necessary connexion. Nothing farther is the case. Contemplate the subject at all sides; you will never find any other origin of that idea.'* (Hume, 1748)

Hume is asserting that the idea of necessary connection is not meaningless, but it does not have the meaning we might have supposed it to have. There is no meaning in the idea that the power is out there in the world – we do not see such power, and with no initiating impression we do not know what we are talking about. The necessary connection is an internal one of 'sentiment' or 'feeling'. In the imagination, when one billiard ball strikes another, the idea of the second moving becomes lively and bold, and belief in its subsequent movement is generated. The only necessity of which we can speak comes from us, not from the world.

Hume's answer to the problem of causation is certainly sceptical, but it is important not to exaggerate the scope of his scepticism. As we have seen, he does not think that the idea of necessary connection is totally devoid of meaning. This means we can still talk of necessary connections and power and energy. But we must recognize that causation, in this sense, is something the human mind brings to our understanding of the world. It is essentially grounded in the expectations which have been forced into us by habit and repetition, to such an extent that we trust those expectations as if they followed some actual law.

Causation as Constant Conjunction

Hume's view is often known as the 'constant conjunction understanding of causation'. It states that all we can properly mean by saying that one thing causes another is that the two events are constantly joined together and so when one happens the mind is naturally forced to the expectation of the second. This second event appears to the mind as inevitable, and this inevitability 'colours' the two events and we shade them together to form a causal union. But, in fact, if we look closely, we just see one event and then another, and that is all.

There is another aspect of Hume's position that is worthy of note. Again, this modifies and subdues his scepticism. In an important sense we 'discover' causation rather then invent it. If all we can properly mean by causation is that two kinds of events are constantly conjoined, it is not us that invents this conjunction of events. The necessity that we feel that is there is our colouring in, but the constant conjunction itself is not.

Science, at least partly, proceeds by way of trying to find these constant conjunctions. In chemistry, for example, we try to discover what regularly happens when one thing is mixed with another. When it happens enough times, we can legitimately say that acid X (for example) causes metal Y to dissolve. But all we can mean by this, says Hume, is that there has been a constant conjunction between the two. We must not try to say that we have seen that one *makes* the other dissolve. We see no such thing. Events follow other events. We come to certain expectations. We cannot help believing that we shall fall from windows. And so we go out the door. That is all.

Inductive Reasoning

This perhaps is the most radical and far-reaching aspect of Hume's scepticism and his underlying thesis that our minds cannot see into the nature of things. First of all, let us briefly explain what we mean by 'induction'. Hume does not use the word 'induction', but the problem he highlighted has become known as the problem of induction, and so it is the word we will use here.

Basically, an 'inductive inference' is when a person goes beyond the present evidence and infers something more general. Hume says he is enquiring about 'the nature of that evidence which assures us of any real existence and matter of fact, beyond the present testimony of our senses, or the records of our memory' (Hume, 1748).

An example of a typical inductive inference will help. Imagine you see a fire burning merrily in a hearth in a distant part of a room. You see the light of the flames. What do you infer will be the case if you were to go near to the fire? Of course, you would infer that near the fire you will feel heat. What would happen if you were to put your hand into the flames? You would infer that you would experience horrible pain. Strictly speaking, in both these inferences, you are going beyond the present evidence of your senses and memory. You are not yet close to the fire, and so are not getting any heat. You might remember getting pain from being too close to a fire, but you have no memory of the *next time* you put your hand too near. That event has not happened.

We use induction all the time. You opened this book expecting the pages to turn because that has been your constant experience of books. You sit in a chair not expecting that it will turn into a porcupine because you have never experienced this. You negotiate the world at every juncture by going beyond the present and thinking 'So far things have been like this and so they will continue to be like this'. The sun has risen every morning, so you think it will rise tomorrow. Induction is like an ever-present and absolutely indispensable companion who is continually telling you what will happen next. Without her constant guidance, you would be utterly lost. Her guidance seems perfectly reasonable and perfectly justified. Hume, however, shows us that there is a seemingly intractable problem at the heart of such inferences.

We first have to note, says Hume, that future events are not completely assured. There is no contradiction in the idea that the sun will not rise tomorrow. It is, therefore, possible for the sun not to rise tomorrow. The only things of which we can be certain are what Hume calls relations of ideas – the ways that concepts **work** together. Three times five will always equal a half of 30. To suppose that it will not is to suppose a contradiction. You are supposing that 15 does not equal 15. The sun not rising tomorrow, in contrast, hasn't any kind of contradiction in it. So it possible for the sun not to rise. Hume calls statements that are not relations of ideas – the ordinary facts that we like to suppose we know – matters of fact.

Now, given that it is possible for the sun not to rise tomorrow, how can we be assured that it will, in (matter of) fact, rise tomorrow? After all, it needn't do. It is also possible for the chair you are sitting on to turn into a porcupine (or a turnip or, more optimistically, a diamond ring worth a lot of money). All this is possible since the ideas do not clash with each other (like supposing that three times five is not equal to 15). Of course, we do not think any of these things are likely. They are distant possibilities, but nevertheless they are possible.

But what justification have we that it is more likely that the sun will rise tomorrow or that the chair will continue to be a chair? Induction is the answer. It has always turned out that way. We might agree that other things can happen, but we think they are unlikely or incredibly remote. Their unlikelihood is due to the fact that they have never happened before or that they have happened only very rarely. We are using induction to work out the possibilities and their probability. We do not even bother to think of remote possibilities like the chair becoming a turnip. Such things have never happened. A chair breaking sometimes happens. It is more probable, although again it is (hopefully) pretty remote.

But now Hume asks the crucial question: What possible justification do we have for relying on induction in our working out the probability of future events? Hume puts it like this:

> *'The bread, which I formerly eat, nourished me; that is, a body of such sensible qualities [i.e. outward appearance – colour, texture...etc] was, at that time, endued with such secret powers: but does it follow, the other bread must nourish me at another time, and the*

like sensible qualities must always be attended with like
secret powers? The consequence seems nowise necessary.'
(Hume, 1748)

We have agreed that the conclusions about matters of fact are not logical proofs like the conclusions of maths (which are relations of ideas), so what can justify the following argument?

Bread nourished me on Thursday.

Bread nourished me on Friday.

Bread nourished me on Saturday

Therefore, bread will continue to nourish me.

What is the exact status of the 'therefore' in this typical inductive inference? It is not a logical and totally safe inference after all (it is 'in nowise necessary'). So what exactly justifies the jump from Saturday, and the other past instances of bread nourishing me, to assurance about the future of bread?

The most obvious answer is that such inferences are justified because such inferences have always worked in the past (or almost always). Yesterday when I ate bread it turned out (yet again) that I was safe in the assumption that it would nourish me. My chair, also, refuses steadfastly to become a turnip or a porcupine and so the inference that it will continue not to do so seems to grow more and more reliable.

We have arrived at this conclusion: induction's past successes, which are enormous in number and growing day by day, surely constitute a massive amount of evidence that induction is a safe kind of inferential move. In other words, I am justified in using induction because of its past successes.

But this answer is hopeless. Hume (who was the first fully to appreciate this) says that to argue like this is to argue in a circle and take 'for granted […] the very point in question' (Hume, 1748). It is to use an inductive inference to justify induction – what logicians call 'begging the question'. We are essentially arguing like this:

Induction worked on Thursday

Induction worked on Friday

Induction worked on Saturday

Therefore induction will continue to work.

But this is an exact parallel to the argument given before, which attempted to justify the belief that bread will continue to nourish me. We simply cannot use the very point which is in question in any justification, but this is exactly what we do if we attempt to justify induction by pointing to its past successes. The past successes are not relevant here. We want justification that we can use induction to justify the inference that the bread will continue to nourish me. But the only way that it appears it can be justified is to point to its past successes. We are caught in a circle.

Induction is not Rational

Hume concludes that we cannot say that induction is justified by reason. Think how radical this conclusion is and how it threatens to undermine the whole fabric of our lives. You are using induction all the time. Every inference about matters of fact which is beyond the present scope of memory and the senses is based on induction. Your beliefs about fire, cooking, football, gardening, your relatives, your own body, and all the other activities of life are crucially dependent upon induction. And yet, Hume shows that induction cannot be rationally justified.

What is the solution? Is there a solution? Again, Hume thinks that ordinary life comes to the rescue. He says that we are so constituted by our nature that we cannot help but believe that things will turn out similarly to how they turned out in the past. Custom and habit – the continued repetition of bread being good for me – entrench an attitude and an expectation about bread. In the same way, we cannot help but believe that gravity will continue to pull me down to the ground, that windows are not as reliable a means of exit as doors. The principle behind our belief that the world will continue is not reason. Hume says,

> *'[the] principle is CUSTOM or HABIT. For wherever the repetition of any particular act or operation produces a propensity to renew the same act or operation, without being impelled by any reasoning or process of the understanding, we always say, that this propensity is the effect of Custom. By employing that word, we pretend not to have given the ultimate reason for such a propensity. We only point out a principle of human nature.'* (Hume, 1748)

We see here a prime example of Hume being the Newton of the mind. Just as Newton had described the ordered mathematical relations between the planets, so Hume shows that the mind orbits its accustomed centres of habit. We might have thought that our minds worked along the lines of logic and God-given reason, but they do not. Instead it is custom and habit that rule. Minds are repelled or attracted by the brute facts of habit. An attitude about bread is entrenched and an idea is then enforced and enlivened until we believe it.

Hume remains modest however. He does not say that this is any kind of ultimate truth about the secret nature of minds. He is just describing what actually happens and, by doing so, trying to clarify the laws of our thinking. But, like Newton, he is framing no hypothesis about the ultimate nature of reality. Our faculties, he says, are narrow and can 'carry us no further' (Hume, 1748). For Hume, it is a simple, but unfortunate fact that our minds haven't the mental acuity to allow us to legitimately frame the kinds of hypotheses that the rationalists insisted could be made.

Today's neuroscientists are finding that Hume was right in describing the brain as seeing causal connections when there may be nothing more than correlation. They describe humans as being 'anticipatory systems' (Rosen, 2012) and note that 'the brain can predict future input by learning about and exploiting statistical regularities in its inputs (de Lange and Kok, 2018) because it is useful. We move effectively through the world by using 'rules of thumb' or heuristics (Kahneman, 2012) that play out, for the most part, as we anticipated. Or as Hume says, 'All our reasonings concerning matter of fact are founded on a species of Analogy, which leads us to expect from any cause the same events' (Hume, 1748).

Why waste time worrying about whether the sun will rise tomorrow, when statistical regularities suggest that it will, and there are plenty of other things to worry about? But at the same time, Hume says, it is still entirely possible that one day it may not.

4. Free Will and Determinism

Hume was particularly proud of his thoughts on the problem of free will. He showed his enthusiasm in a short summary of the *Treatise* that he wrote shortly after its publication. 'The whole controversy', he tells us, will be put in 'a new light, by giving a new definition to necessity.' (This is from the Abstract of the *Treatise*, which Hume published shortly after the publication of the *Treatise*. It can be found in Millican, 2002a). Hume definitely thinks he has something new to say about an old problem – and it is a problem that has long haunted philosophers, theologians and anyone who has seriously stopped to consider their place in the world of nature and material stuff. Let's examine the problem first, and then look at Hume's solution.

We think of ourselves as free beings – we think that, if we are of sound mind, we are able to determine our actions. If the circumstances are right, we are able to decide what to do. For example, it may be that you chose this book instead of spending your money on something less worthy. Unless there was a gun to your head or you have a particular compulsion to buy books on Hume, you think that the action of buying the book was not compulsive or necessary. In other words, you decided freely. It was your choice.

In fact, we think that this freedom to choose is so significant that we say that people who choose freely are morally responsible for their actions. Take, for example, a situation where you accidentally tread on my foot. I will not blame you even though you hurt me. This is because I do not think you chose to do it. But if you were to do it deliberately, I would resent the action and blame you. Why do I blame you? Because the action came freely out of you – it was something you chose to do. I hold you morally accountable for your freely chosen action. It seems that free will or deliberate choice is necessary for moral blame to be appropriate.

Imagine the consequences if we found out that actually all that has ever happened is necessary and pre-determined – that there isn't (and there never has been) any real choice over anything that happened. If this were the case, surely free will would be an illusion. It seems blame and holding people morally responsible would be completely inappropriate. Suppose that I found out that your 'deliberate' action was in fact something you had no choice over. I would still have a hurt foot, but it seems now I have to think of you as not guilty of anything. I would have to say that you had no choice. The action was forced out of you. There would be no way that you could have stopped it. Surely then I cannot blame you.

It is hard to imagine a world where people do not have free will. This kind of world would be a very weird and alien one. However, the big problem in the 'free will and necessity' debate is that this appears to be exactly the kind of world we inhabit. It seems there can't be any such thing as free will. It seems that liberty and choice are illusions. After all, human beings are material beings with material bodies and brains – all of which obey the laws of physics. If this is right, the laws of physics determine what happens, not you.

Many philosophers of Hume's time certainly thought like this. Many were rigid determinists. This determinism came in two varieties. Some thought that it is just a natural fact that 'causes necessitate their effects'. Others were determinists for religious reasons. They believed that God has created a world where all events are made to happen by the divine will. Everything is therefore pre-determined by God. For example, some people are made for hell, while others (much more fortunate) are destined for heaven. This frightening doctrine was very popular in Hume's era and was known as 'predestination'. Believers in predestination thought that every event in the world is caused to happen by a previous event – the effect flows from the cause inevitably, remorselessly. No different effect can occur from that cause. Just as one domino necessitates the fall of the second, so every event just happens with inexorable, deterministic inevitability. Since human beings inhabit this world and are composed of the same matter as everything else, they too are part of this rigid causal order.

Transcending Natural Law

There might be a way out of the problem if we think of ourselves as somehow transcending the laws of nature. If we think of ourselves as somehow mirroring God and being made in God's image, rather than being like other living beings such as a tree or a dog, we can see ourselves – as humans – as special in some supernatural way. From this perspective, human beings are 'above' the ordinary course of nature and are therefore able to set things in motion as a first free cause, in the same way that God can.

As we have seen, however, the option of taking that perspective was becoming increasingly remote in Hume's time. The Enlightenment project viewed the human person as much more down to earth – a natural rather than a supernatural inhabitant – a part and parcel of the whole. As a completely natural being, humankind is subject to the same laws of nature as anything else. Leaves fall from trees necessarily due to the effects of decay and gravity, and while humans are much more complex than leaves, the necessity of their movements is essentially the same. We too are fated to flutter, fade and die as parts of the immensely complex, completely natural, causal order.

Hume's Solution

Hume thinks he sees a way out of the problem – a way of bringing together how we think of events as necessary and the way we think of human beings as free. In Section 8 of the *Enquiry*, he explores the ideas of 'Liberty and Necessity'. Hume tells us that he has in mind a 'reconciling project with regard to the question of liberty and necessity'. He thinks he can reduce the problem to little more than a quibble about terminology:

> '*it will not require many words to prove, that all mankind have ever agreed in the doctrine of liberty as well as in that of necessity, and that the whole dispute, in this respect also, has been merely verbal.*' (Hume, 1748)

What then does all mankind agree on with regard to liberty or freedom of will? First, liberty does not mean randomness.

A sudden, inexplicable burst of energy from us that results in a completely unpredictable jerk or spasm is not really free. A truly voluntary action flows from people's character and motives with a certain degree of predictability and naturalness. Human behaviour is predictable, not random. Hume gives some amusing examples to show this:

> *'Were a man, whom I know to be honest and opulent, and with whom I live in intimate friendship, to come to my house, where I am surrounded by my servants, I rest assured, that he is not to stab me before he leaves it, in order to rob me of my silver standish; and I no more suspect this event, than the falling down of my house itself, which is new, and solidly built and founded... A man who at noon leaves his purse full of money on the pavement at Charing Cross, may as well expect that it will fly away like a feather, as that he will find it untouched an hour after.'* (Hume, 1748)

We can rely on honest people we know well not to murder us. We can rely on other people's dishonesty if we are foolish enough to leave temptation in their path. This means that we are already prepared to accept a certain degree of necessity in the actions of people. A good, honest friend 'necessarily' will not murder me. The purse full of money 'necessarily' won't be there if it is left for a certain amount of time at one the busiest thoroughfares in London.

Someone might protest that human behaviour is not predictable with 100 per cent reliability. But, Hume replies, this is also true of the natural world: 'a sudden earthquake [...] [may] arise, and shake and tumble my house about my ears' (Hume, 1748).

Both human behaviour and the natural world exhibit reliable and regular patterns of movement. When there is something unpredictable or strange, we think that this strangeness can also be explained by causes we have not taken into account or realized were there. If a person who is normally polite and gentle were to give a rude answer to a question, we might find that his irritability is explained by the fact that he has 'toothache or has not dined' (Hume, 1748). Strange behaviour is to be accounted for by causes that we know nothing about – once we know these unguessed causes, we see the normal flow of cause and effect.

What Hume is trying to do here is show that events in the natural world and actions in the world of human affairs are on a par. They are both predictable, and when they appear random it is due to some underlying unknown causes.

A Different Kind of Necessity

We usually understand events in the natural world as being necessary – for instance, if you open your hand then it appears the things you are holding will necessarily drop to the floor. In the same way, I can say that the person who is my friend necessarily will not murder me. The dropping to the floor is necessary given that I open my hand; my friend's honesty and genial behaviour is necessary given his lovely character. The moral that Hume wants to draw is that there is an equivalence of necessity here.

But then what about liberty or freedom? What does it mean to say that an agent is acting freely? Again, Hume thinks that everyone has always agreed on what it is to be free. Liberty, he says, means being able to do what you want to do – to not have your behaviour impeded by exterior forces:

'By *liberty, then, we can only mean a power of acting or not acting, according to the determinations of the will; that is, if we choose to remain at rest, we may; if we choose to move, we also may. Now this hypothetical liberty is universally allowed to belong to everyone, who is not a prisoner and in chains. Here then is no subject of dispute.'* (Hume, 1748)

If you want to move, but are tied to a chair or paralyzed by fear, then we will all agree that you are not free. You cannot do what you want to do. If, however, you are able to move and choose to do so, then you are free.

So there are two ideas which Hume thinks can be reconciled if we have a proper understanding of the meaning of the terms involved. First, the idea that human behaviour is regular, and in that sense, as necessary as the events that happen in the natural world. Second, the idea that freedom is not chance – freedom exists where your motives and desires can reliably result in action that is not prevented by external forces like prison walls. You want to move. You move. That's freedom.

Little of what Hume has said would have been particularly novel or new to the thinkers of his day, so what 'new light' is he proposing to shine upon the reconciling project? The answer, he tells us in his Abstract to the *Treatise*, lies in his position upon the nature of necessity. In Chapter 3 we examined Hume's solution to the meaning of terms like 'necessity', 'power', 'force' and the like. Let's recap what Hume said.

Most of us imagine that when we see a hurtling stone and then a broken window there was some necessitating energy that the stone delivered to the window – a force making it break. Hume argues that we cannot really mean this since there is nothing in this conjunction of events that we can recognize as the necessitating force. We do not see the stone make the window break – strictly speaking, all we observe is that a stone moves and the window breaks when the stone makes contact. One event certainly follows another event and there is contact, but do we observe 'making'?

So what can we mean by necessity? Recall that, according to Hume's Copy Principle (see Chapter 3), it is impossible for an expression to have meaning unless we have some sensory input – some 'impression' as Hume calls it. The blind man who has never seen blue cannot truly understand a description of the sky as being blue. For him the word is a kind of blank.

Hume proposes that all we can mean by necessity in the context of cause and effect is to do with an internal feeling, a feeling that gathers liveliness due to repetition. Windows have regularly broken when impacted by stones of a certain size and weight. We 'feel' – have an expectation – that the second billiard ball will move when the hurtling cue ball hits it.

This 'constant conjunction' results in a feeling of necessity, but this is in us – our minds – not in the world outside our bodies, since we do not observe this necessity in the world itself. All we have is eventual obedient expectation bludgeoned into us by the brute force of repeated instances. It is all habituated expectation, not some kind of supernatural insight into the secret reality of the ways that things work.

This, then, is the force of the word 'necessity' when we say that motives necessitate actions or that leaves are 'made' to fall to the ground in autumn. Hume tells us: 'Beyond the constant conjunction of similar objects, and the consequent inference from one to the other, we have no notion of necessity, or connexion' (Hume, 1748).

All we mean by necessity, then, is that there has been a regular pattern of certain events of type A followed by certain events of type B. So when we say that, given a person's character the action was necessary, all we are actually saying is that people of this type regularly do actions of that sort. Therefore, Hume says, 'it must follow that all mankind have ever agreed in the doctrine of necessity' (1748). In other words, if we think about it, we see that we have always agreed that this is so. We have always observed that people of a certain character regularly produce actions of certain types. We predict what people do. In exactly the same way, we predict what will happen in the world of nature as well. If a billiard ball hits another, we predict movement.

What then is the 'new light' in the understanding of necessity that Hume is bringing to this debate? It is his less forceful view of what 'necessity' encompasses. It is not the full-blown necessity which is built into the structure of things – an external, objective necessity. It is not a necessity which compels or forces its result. Necessity is not like this. All we mean, indeed, all we can mean, is that there has been a reliable pattern of events, which has created an internal feeling of expectation. This kind of necessity, Hume argues, is nothing to worry about since we have always known about it and accepted it as part of what we mean by free action.

Determinism is Needed

In his famous essay 'The Dilemma of Determinism' (1884), the philosopher and psychologist William James

(1842–1910) classified various responses to determinism (the idea that everything in nature is necessitated by a cause or a cause necessitates its effect). A philosopher who thinks that determinism results in there being no such thing as free will is called a 'hard determinist'. On the other hand, a philosopher who thinks determinism is compatible with free will is called a 'soft determinist' (or 'compatibilist'). Under this classification, Hume is a soft determinist or compatibilist. He thinks, as we have seen, that you can have free will and you can have determinism. Remember, his is a 'reconciling project' (the only disagreement here might be with those who think that Hume is not a full-blooded determinist because he does not accept that there is a necessary connection between cause and effect).

Since James' useful distinction, there have been some further developments in philosophy. Some determinists have gone further than just saying that determinism is compatible with the existence of freedom. They think that determinism has to be true if people are going to be free. Their basic argument is that the only alternative to determinism is indeterminism, which is just chance, but mere randomness cannot provide a stable basis for freedom.

A person who thinks that determinism is actually needed for there to be freedom, has come to be known as a hard compatibilist. Such a person is saying more than just 'free will and determinism can co-exist'; he or she is saying that one cannot exist without the other – freedom relies upon determinism being true. This appears to be what Hume is saying in the *Enquiry*. Necessity (determinism), he says, is 'not only consistent with morality, but absolutely essential to its support'. But then why do we blame people for actions? Hume answers this question by saying that it is not so much the action that is blameworthy, but the character behind the action. Actions, he says, only last a short amount of time – they are 'temporary and perishing'. If you stand deliberately upon my foot, it is not the standing on the foot that is so much the problem, but the character that led you to do it.

Why don't we blame people for actions which they did not do deliberately? Because, says Hume, such actions are not reliable indicators of the kind of character which led to the action. We do not know what kind of person someone is from an action which is done out of ignorance or by accident. In contrast, an action done deliberately does indicate the kind of character you are. If you deliberately stand on people's feet then you are unkind.

But in order to know this, there has to be reliability – and only a stable system of constant conjunction can allow this. Hume explains that 'actions render a person criminal, merely as they are proofs of criminal principles in the mind [i.e. character] [...] except upon the doctrine of necessity, they never were just proofs and never were criminal' (Hume, 1748). In other words, unless certain actions are reliable indicators (proofs) of certain characters, there is no point in punishment and blame. We could never know what a person is like, or describe them as such-and-such a kind of person, if their character produced random actions; reliable blame would be impossible. Therefore, necessity is not only compatible with freedom, it is required.

Is Hume Right?

Hume defines freedom as the ability to do what you want. Most would agree that this is certainly part of what we mean by freedom, but a lot of scholars think that more than this is required. They accuse Hume of an inadequate, too-weak notion of what it is to be free. One counter to Hume goes along the following lines. Imagine Larry, a happy and fulfilled kleptomaniac. Although his compulsion makes him steal things, he is quite happy to be like that. He likes nothing better than to steal things. Is Larry free?

Most people want to say that Larry is not free. He cannot help but steal since he has a compulsion. Note, however, that according to Hume's definition of freedom, Larry is free. After all, he is doing what he wants. He is not in prison (yet). He is not in chains. He has a desire to steal and goes out and does it. In that case, according to Hume, he is a free agent. However, many would think that Larry is not free despite doing what he wants to do. He is, after all, a victim of compulsion. So is being able to do what you want really sufficient for freedom? That's one concern about Hume's account, but there is a more significant one.

The other problem arises from our belief that in order to say that someone is free, they have to be able to do otherwise. If we found out that your stepping on my foot was deliberate, but there was no chance of you doing otherwise, I'd be in some doubt as to whether or not you could be truly blamed. I would question whether you were really free.

If determinism is true, however, then there is no alternative. Everything that happens has no real chance of not happening. Everything I am writing now was fixed in advance by the way the universe has evolved. Cause upon cause has necessitated its own individual effect. Those effects have come to give birth to their own individual effects. If this is true, it means that every event was written into the very fabric of the universe once the Big Bang had occurred and sent out its causal emissaries.

The force of this objection is not diminished if we accept Hume's less forceful account of necessity. According to Hume's necessity we cannot say that the events were 'written' into the fabric of the universe (because we can observe no such writing). But surely it would be enough to say that we expect or feel that every action has no real alternative.

But for freedom it seems there has to be a real chance of alternatives – the possibility of genuine choice. If John gets to a fork in the road, and he chooses the left-hand side, is he really free if that was the only side he could have chosen? True, he is doing what he wants, but is he genuinely free if the other choice was not really available to him? Many people think that, in order for there to be freedom, we have to have genuine alternatives.

Hume acknowledges this criticism when he says:

> *'I pretend not to have obviated or removed all objections to this theory, with regard to necessity and liberty. I can foresee other objections [...] It may be said, for instance, that, if voluntary actions be subjected to the same laws of necessity with the operations of matter, there is a continued chain of necessary causes, pre-ordained and pre-determined, reaching from the original cause of all, to every single volition of every human creature. No contingency any where in the universe; no indifference, no liberty.'* (Hume, 1748)

Hume does not seem to have an answer to the objection that he foresees. Perhaps he thinks that as long as we can do what we want, that is all we can reasonably require in terms of having freedom. True, your wants and character are something over which you have no real power. They were formed by causes outside yourself and there was no real chance of you being anything other than what you became.

Today, probably the majority of philosophers accept Hume's 'reconciling project'. They may disagree on the details, but they are compatibilists. They believe that determinism and freedom do not contradict each other. We are still governed by the principles put forward in the Enlightenment. Human beings are just a part of nature. They are governed by the laws of physics. The consequence appears to be that the only kind of freedom that we can have is the type that Hume puts forward. If we can do what we want, that is enough. Yes, the world is determined, but this determinism does not imply that you cannot do what you want. It only implies that what you want is inevitable given the way the universe is.

5. Emotions, Reason and Morality

What do you have to do to be morally good? One traditional answer is that being good means following the commands of reason and ignoring the temptations of the emotions. For example, let us imagine that you desire cake and there is a delightful, rich fudge cake on the table in front of you. You have a strong, emotional yearning for its soft, palatable deliciousness. You begin to reach for the cake. What might stop you doing this?

According to the traditional picture, reason could play the role of moderating your cake-eating behaviour. Reason steps in and reminds you of the cake's unhealthiness and calorific content. You are now in a moral quandary. Should you follow the lures of hot, impassioned desire, or do you instead obey the calm pronouncements of reason? The traditional answer is that, in order to be moral, you ought to obey reason. The hot desire of passion is regarded as a sure path to immorality while the cool commands of reason are good.

Hume starts one of his most famous sections of his *Treatise of Human Nature* – Book 2, Part 3 – describing this picture of morality. This section is entitled 'Of the Will and Direct Passions' although we might see it more simply as 'Emotion Vs. Reason'.

He writes:

> *'Nothing is more usual in philosophy, and even in
> common life, than to talk of the combat of passion and
> reason, to give the preference to reason, and assert that
> men are only so far virtuous as they conform themselves
> to its dictates. Every rational creature, 'tis said, is obliged
> to regulate his actions by reason.'*

(By the word 'passion', Hume means any emotion or desire.
The word 'passion' nowadays means something hot-headed, but
for Hume, there can be calm passions like love of life or kindness
to children.)

Hume says that in this kind of approach, reason is praised for
its 'eternity, invariableness and divine origin', while emotion is
accused of 'blindness, unconstancy and deceitfulness'. In other
words, the dispassionate, God-like voice of reason must battle
with the blind foolishness of the emotions. The Emotion Vs.
Reason picture is a powerful one, and still dominates in popular
culture and philosophy to this day.

Hume, as we have so often seen, argues that the traditional
picture is wrong. Reason, he says, cannot battle with the passions.
He argues that the traditional understanding gives reason far too
much power. In Hume's view, we are much more dominated by
passion than we might think. His crucial point is that reason can
never prompt us into action. It is never sufficient, on its own, to
give impulse to an action. It might regulate action, but it cannot
initiate it.

Let us go back to the cake example to see how this works.
You see a cake and a desire forms for the cake since you like

the taste. This 'passion' or desire for the cake is what prompts you to a possible action. You might then reach for the cake and eat it. According to the traditional Emotion Vs. Reason picture, what might happen now is that reason informs you of the cake's unhealthiness, and this simple fact is potentially powerful enough on its own to enable you to resist the cake. Hume disagrees. His sceptical question is this: 'Can reason really motivate a person?'

In other words, what could possibly impel someone to follow the advice of reason? Why would the mere belief 'The cake is unhealthy' make someone stop eating the cake unless they have a desire to remain healthy or stick to their diet? Hume insists that reason, on its own, cannot motivate anyone to do anything – it always has to be joined or accompanied by an emotion, desire or passion since it's always these that are the real impulses to action.

Reason as the Servant of Desire

In Hume's alternative picture – which we might reasonably call the Passion Vs. Passion picture – reason simply informs the agent whether a statement is true or false. Reason, for Hume, is the truth-deciding faculty of the mind. It tries to work out what beliefs we should have. But Hume says that the mind has more than one faculty; the mind also contains many desires and passions competing for attention. However, without any beliefs about the world, all these competing impulses to action do not know where to go. The site of competing passions and desires we can call the 'passion faculty'. Reason's job is to supply (potentially) true beliefs to this passion faculty.

Let us suppose, for example, that a belief comes in from the reason faculty – 'There is cake on the table'. The passion faculty contains a desire for cake, and so you reach for the cake because of the passion. Let us suppose that you also have other desires in the passion faculty. You want to keep on your diet. You want to be slimmer. Another belief arrives from reason: 'Cakes are unhealthy'. What do you now do? Do you follow the passion for cake or the passion for slimness?

In Hume's Passion Vs. Passion picture, it depends upon the relative strength of the passions involved. If your desire for cake is stronger than your passion for slimness then you reach for the cake. If your desire to keep to your diet is stronger, you will not reach for the cake. Your passions will determine what you will do.

Reason, in Hume's picture of the mind, is simply the servant of the passions – it is always the supplier of beliefs, not the impulse to action.

One of Hume's most quoted sentences comes from this section of the *Treatise*: 'Reason is, and ought to be, the slave of the passions, and can never pretend to any other office than to serve and obey them.' (The phrase 'ought to be' is usually interpreted as a rhetorical flourish rather than a philosophical assertion. If we were to take it seriously, it would seem to flout one of Hume's own rules that an 'ought' cannot be derived from an 'is'. We will be looking at this later in the chapter.)

We can look at this from another angle using Hume's experimental method. Find a belief in your reasoning faculty (that is to say, a rational belief). Suppose it is the belief that Paris is the capital of France. Here you note a particular relationship between two ideas: 'Paris' and 'France'. What actions does the noticing of this relationship prompt you to perform? According to Hume, there will be no motivation to action whatsoever. You will simply notice a belief – a statement about a particular relationship floats before your mind's eye. It will be motivationally inert. However, let us suppose that, contrary to Hume's expectation, the statement 'Paris is the capital of France' seems to provide you with a strong motivation to go there.

What would Hume say if that happened? Hume would ask you to examine the impulse a bit closer. Is it really just the belief that gives you the impulse to go to Paris or, for instance, your memory of the pleasures of Paris? Perhaps you have never been there, but have seen alluring pictures of its architectural delights. Hume insists that it is really your emotional response to the memories or pictures that is driving you in the direction of going to Paris.

Hume is confident that you will always find, under closer inspection, that the mere presence of information cannot, on its own, supply any impetus to action. Experiment all you want, he says, and you will discover that any motivation is always sparked by a passion. Reason has a role, but a subservient one. The reasoning faculty can only step in to provide you with the relevant beliefs that will help you negotiate a way to the fulfilment of your desires. Reason is the helper or organizer. Under the direction of the passions, reason finds the best means available for you to get what you want.

For Hume it is vitally important that we realize that passion is the wellspring of our actions. We must realize that we are not God-like beings who can employ reason in a dispassionate sense. Reason's role is subsidiary. This is not to say that it has no role whatsoever. As we have seen, it regulates behaviour, but the real drives we possess are those that reside in the passion faculty.

No Passion is Unreasonable

There is a vitally important consequence to this Passion Vs. Passion picture of motivation. Hume defines passion like this in Book 2 of the *Treatise*:

> *'A passion is an original existence, or, if you will, modification of existence, and contains not any representative quality, which renders it a copy of any other existence or modification. When I am angry, I am actually possest with the passion, and in that emotion have no more reference to any other object, than when I am thirsty, or sick, or more than five foot high.'*
> (Hume, 1739)

What does Hume mean by this? Basically, he is saying that an emotion does not represent a thing in the world. If I am angry or sad or jealous, the emotion itself is not true or false. Typically, it is a reaction to the world, rather than a representation of it. Of course, it is true or false that you have the emotion (we can lie about how we are feeling), but the emotion itself is not true or false. It is, as philosophers like to say, 'non-cognitive'. It is not the kind of thing that is capable of being true or false.

The non-cognitive nature of the passions contrasts with the cognitive nature of beliefs. It is quite sensible to ask if a belief is true or false. For example, the belief that the moon is made of cheese is false. In stark contrast, it is silly to ask whether anger is true or false. You simply have the emotion – it simply exists; it is not a representation of existence. It is, to use Hume's terminology, a 'modification of existence' (a different way of being). A belief can be true or false since it does try to represent something about the external world. The belief that Paris is the capital of France represents the way things are correctly, and so the belief is true. The belief 'the cat is on the mat' is true if the cat is on the mat. However, a desire, emotion, or passion does not represent anything else – it is simply there. It modifies what you feel like.

If passions do not represent something else and are therefore neither true nor false, then there is a very important consequence. We often think of some passions as unreasonable or even totally mad. A desire to throw an elephant is unreasonable since it is impossible for a human to throw an elephant. We think that anyone who fears leprechauns is deluded since there are no leprechauns. Hume agrees that, in so far as these passions are founded on false beliefs, they are unreasonable. However, it is the false belief that is unreasonable, not the passion. The passion itself, strictly speaking, is incapable of being unreasonable. Why? Because it is simply there as something affecting our psychology. Remember the fear – the feeling itself – does not represent anything. It is not, in itself, true or false. How can something that is neither true nor false be unreasonable? Only the belief that might accompany the passion can be unreasonable since beliefs are capable of being true or false. Questions and commands, for example, are non-cognitive. A question like 'What is the weather like?' is not the kind of thing which is true or false. It does not express a fact; it asks for one. Similarly, a command like 'Open the door' is non-cognitive.

Hume expresses this idea with deliberate comedy: 'Tis not contrary to reason to prefer the destruction of the whole world to the scratching of my finger' (Hume, 1739). If I have this preference, it is simply a desire I happen to have. 'Tis as little contrary to reason to prefer even my own acknowledg'd lesser good to my greater, and have a more ardent affection for the former than for the latter', he continues. The only way that we might say that it is unreasonable is if it is founded on a false belief. Hume summarizes his ideas by saying, 'In short, a passion must be accompany'd with some false judgment, in order to its being unreasonable; and even then 'tis not the passion, properly speaking, which is unreasonable, but the judgment' (Hume, 1739).

Reason or Calm Passion?

Hume further examines the Emotion Vs. Reason picture in order to point out another of its deficiencies. When we realize that a passion is unreasonable, in the sense that it is founded on a false belief, there is no struggle between calm reason and insistent, hot-headed passion – the kind of struggle that the Reason Vs. Emotion picture encourages us to imagine exists. Immediately when reason informs us that the passion is based upon a falsehood, the passion just yields 'to our reason without any opposition. I may desire any fruit as of an excellent relish [i.e. think that something is going to be pleasurable]; but whenever you convince me of my mistake, my longing ceases' (Hume, 1739). To use a different example: if you are afraid that there are monsters under the bed, but then become convinced (by reason) that there are no monsters under the bed, the fear immediately ceases. (If you continue to fear, it is only because you are not totally convinced that there are no monsters lurking there.)

However, let us ask a question. Why is it that it feels like there are battles for control within us? It certainly feels like reason sometimes has to struggle with emotions. To return to the cake example – doesn't it feel like reason battles with your desire for the cake's taste? You run through the facts as you contemplate the cake. 'The cake is high in calories.' 'The cake is unhealthy.' 'I am on a diet.' These are the voices of reason, but the facts fail to subdue the desire for the cake. You agonize. Surely this is reason battling with the emotions.

Hume acknowledges that there are times when it feels like this, but it is still a mistake to think that reason struggles with the passions. Reason, says Hume, is calm. It 'exerts itself without producing any sensible emotion' (Hume, 1739). Reason just gives you the facts calmly and there is no particular feel to its delivery. This contrasts with many emotions. For example, when you are angry, you feel hot and bothered. However, there are emotions that are similar to reason in having a lack of distinctive, inner feel. These are the calm, tranquil emotions.

When it feels like reason battles with the emotions, it is really these calm emotions doing battle with the hot-headed ones. Because they are the calm ones, and reason is also calm, we mistakenly think that it is reason that battles for control. It is as if the emotions disguise themselves as reason. However, in Hume's Passion Vs. Passion picture, the only way that there can be inner struggle between competing claims for control is if a passion engages another passion.

Again an inner experiment can be performed. Think through the cake example. The desires for the pleasures of eating are often not particularly calm. Indeed, eating cake is, for all too many of us, a fervently passionate activity. Being on a diet, and its accompanying desires (to be thinner, to be healthier, to eat in moderation) are much calmer. They are peaceful, tranquil desires. A desire for moderation can hardly be violent. So when the calmness of the dieting desire comes up against the passion for delicious cake, it feels like calm reason is wrestling with the passion for cake. It is not so. The calm desire for dieting quietly battles with the shrill shouts of our cake desires.

Morality Does Not Stem From Reason

In Hume's time, many philosophers held to a firmly rationalist picture of morality. One of its principal advocates was Samuel Clarke (1675–1729) who wrote *A Discourse Concerning the Unchangeable Obligations of Natural Religion, and the Truth and Certainty of the Christian Revelation* (first printed in 1706). Clarke says that moral truths are fixed, eternal and necessary. Moreover, they are discoverable through reason. Just as it is foolish to assert that a crooked line is a straight one, it is rationally impossible to deny that certain actions are good and others are bad. The badness and goodness of certain actions are fixed and plainly discernible – in fact, Clarke says, the goodness or badness is as plain and obvious as the rising of the sun or simple arithmetic. It is theories such as these that Hume opposed. His principal reason for thinking this is familiar: reason cannot perform the task. It is too weak for the job.

Hume's first argument is simple, and takes off from the principle we discussed earlier. Reason cannot on its own, initiate any action. It is motivationally inert. Morality, on the other hand, is practical. It is about inspiring us or motivating us to do certain things and refraining from others. But if morality is action-initiating, and reason cannot be, then reason cannot be the origin of morality. Hume puts it like this:

'Since morals, therefore, have an influence on our actions and affections, it follows that they cannot be deriv'd from reason; and that because reason alone, as we have already prov'd, can never have any such influence. Morals excite passions, and produce or prevent actions. Reason of itself is utterly impotent in this particular. The rules of morality, therefore, are not conclusions of reason.' (Hume, 1739)

In other words, morality is inspirational. It enlivens us into action. The motive of kindness, for example, prompts us to help people. The ethic of justice prompts us to seek a fairer distribution of goods. Reason, on the other hand, simply finds out and informs us whether a statement is true or false. Given the two very different roles, morality cannot be derived from reason.

Hume employs a variety of arguments to bolster his claim that reason is not the source of morality. We will limit ourselves to one of them since it has been very influential especially in recent ethical thought. It has become known as the 'is–ought gap' (or the 'fact–value distinction').

We have seen that reason's job is to discern truth from falsehood. It supplies the passion faculty of the mind with appropriate beliefs so it can perform the job of fulfilling desires. It tells us what is true. Hume complains that often a moral theorist will begin by establishing some truth claim. They will, for example, start with proving that God exists or what human beings are like. Take, for example, the statement that 'humans like to work in groups'. This is an example of an 'is' statement, as is the statement that God exists:

- It is true that God exists.

- It is true that humans like to work in groups.

But then, says Hume, quite often a strange thing happens. Instead of finding further statements in the language of 'is' we find the moral theorist jumping to another kind of statement. They start using 'ought' statements.

- We ought to do God's will.

- We ought to work in groups.

But how on earth do we get from an 'is' to an 'ought'? It seems entirely illogical. Hume says that this jump is imperceptible but vitally important.

> *'For as this ought, or ought not, expresses some new relation or affirmation, 'tis necessary that it be should be observed and explained; and at the same time that a reason should be given, for what seem inconceivable, how this new relation can be a* deduction *from others, which are entirely different from it.'* (Hume, 1739, author's emphasis)

Deduction is one of reason's principal tools. Using it properly, a person is able to think their way to the logical consequences of a statement. For example, what can I legitimately and logically infer (or deduce) from the following statement: 'A man called John is wearing a Hi-Viz jacket on the side of the road'?

What is absolutely guaranteed to be true if this statement is true? I can safely deduce that there is a man called John. There is a Hi-Viz jacket. There is a road. There is a side to the road.

All these are entirely safe, logical deductions. I can probably guess that John is a Highway Agency official, but this is not a deduction – it's just a guess. It is probable, based on other beliefs that I have, but may or may not be true. After all, John could be an ordinary driver who has broken down and has sensibly donned a Hi-Viz jacket.

Deductions are logically safe. But a move from 'is' to 'ought' is never a deduction, according to Hume, so it is never logically safe. The jump from the one to the other needs to be explained. Why should the bare facts logically or deductively lead to ought-statements? Again, what Hume is trying to establish is that morality is not derived from reason. We cannot just look at the facts that reason provides and then from there deduce (using reason) what we ought to do. There is a gap, a leap. There seems to be no safe, logical bridge from one side to the other.

This is a radical conclusion. If Hume is right then, from the facts of the Holocaust, for example, you cannot logically derive its evil. If you saw a group of people setting fire to a cat outside your house, you would feel horror, but you would not be able to work out that their actions are bad (example from Miller, 2003). For Hume, the facts are in one area, and the values seem to be in another.

The Real Origin of Morality

We can now ask the question: 'If morality is not derived from reason, what is its origin?' Hume has an answer. Morality is derived, not from reason, but a different mental faculty altogether. Reason cannot discern the difference between good and bad, so there is a different mental faculty that is the origin of the distinction. There is, Hume says in Book 3, Section 1 of the *Treatise*, a moral sense (a sense of morality, we might say). One of the most important influences for Hume on this topic was Francis Hutcheson (1694–1746), who wrote *An Essay on the Nature and Conduct of the Passions, with Illustrations on the Moral Sense* (1728). Hutcheson was a prominent member of the sentimentalist school of moral philosophy, who opposed the rationalism of philosophers like Clarke. Hutcheson also claimed that we have a moral sense, but what Hume means by a moral sense seems to be very different from Hutcheson. For Hutcheson, the moral sense is analogous to our ordinary senses, but instead of discerning colours, tastes, smells and so on, the moral sense discerns goodness and badness. Hume seems to see the moral sense as entirely explained by our natural feeling towards certain types of action. He explains that when we see certain actions we feel a sense of unease, while when we see other kinds of action, we find agreeable sentiments growing in us. Certain actions make us feel good and certain actions make us feel bad.

> '*There is no spectacle so fair and beautiful as a noble or generous action; nor any which gives us more abhorrence than one that is cruel and treacherous [...] To have this sense of virtue is nothing but to feel a satisfaction of a particular kind from the contemplation of a character. This very feeling constitutes our praise or admiration.*'
> (Hume, 1739)

Here Hume appears to be saying that in mind-independent reality there are no moral facts. Another passage from the same section of the *Treatise* seems to confirm this:

'Take any action allowed to be vicious: Wilful murder,
for instance. Examine it in all lights, and see if you can
find that matter of fact, or real existence, which you call
vice [...] There is no other matter of fact in the case.
The vice entirely escapes you, as long as you consider
the object. You never can find it, till you turn your
reflexion into your own breast, and find a sentiment of
disapprobation, which arises in you, towards this action.
Here is a matter of fact; but 'tis the object of feeling, not of
reason. It lies in yourself, not in the object. So that when
you pronounce any action or character to be vicious, you
mean nothing, but that from the constitution of your
nature you have a feeling or sentiment of blame from
the contemplation of it.' (Hume, 1739)

Morality, it appears, consists entirely in feelings of approval and disapproval. In this reading of Hume, he is really claiming that when we say that 'Justice is good' we are saying no more than 'Justice! Hooray!' (because it fills us with a sense of something like joy). Similarly, when we say 'Murder is wrong' we are really saying no more than 'Murder! Boo!' because it fills us with an uncomfortable feeling. (In the 20th century, this view of ethics was known as 'emotivism'. Its less formal name was the 'Boo! Hoorah! Theory of Ethics'.) Morality amounts to a record of feeling like or dislike towards certain actions and types of character. What this appears to be claiming is that there is absolutely nothing wrong in the actions associated with murder. Hume says, 'The vice entirely escapes you' and the vice 'lies in yourself, not in the object' (Hume 1739).

This has some unfortunate implications. If morality is nothing but attitudes of approval and disapproval, then it appears there is nothing objectively wrong about slavery for example. After all, many societies certainly approved of the practice. They appeared to be expressing shouts of approval: 'Slavery! Hooray!' Relatively recently, we have replaced the expressions of approval for expressions of disgust ('Slavery! Boo!').

The problem is that most of us think that we were right to change our minds and move from approval to disgust. Why? Because we believe that there is something deeply wrong about slavery. Our minds were morally confused or deluded when we thought of it as acceptable. But if there is actually nothing in slavery itself which is wrong, then it is hard to see in what logical sense we were morally deluded.

Fortunately, there are other less sceptical ways of looking at Hume's moral philosophy. Other passages in his writings seem to lead in a different direction, and so some philosophers see Hume as an early forerunner of what is now called quasi-realism. This tries to take seriously the idea that there are no mind-independent moral facts, but rejects the implication that moral judgments cannot be wrong. To understand quasi-realism properly, we have to understand projectivism, so we will look at both of these in the following section.

Projectivism and Quasi-Realism

When a projector throws out a picture onto a screen, in one sense the picture is not real. It has no physical mass – it is not like a painting or photograph that you can carry around with you. If you try to peel off the image cast by the projector, you will end up with a scratched screen. You will have no picture, just a lot of disappointment. In one sense then, the picture on the screen is not real. It is only a projection.

However, there is another sense in which the picture is real. Everyone with normal vision will agree what the picture looks like. For example, if a projector casts the image of the Eiffel Tower, just about everyone will agree with what is being seen. The projection is more than a mere hallucination. This mixture of the unreality of the projection and the reality of people's agreement about the character of the projection explains the name of the theory: quasi-realism.

In this way of understanding Hume, he takes a similar position with regard to morality. When someone sees certain actions, it makes them feel a certain way. This feeling makes them see the action in a certain light. They project their own feeling outward onto the action. For example, when people see an act of extreme generosity – say the sacrifice of someone's life for another – they feel a certain way about the action. It fills them with feelings of approval and admiration. This makes them see the action in a certain way. The sacrificial act is bathed in the light of a warm inner glow. When someone sees an act of treachery, a different colouring appears. The disgust you feel is transferred outward onto the action. It now wears the appearance of wrongness.

Now, in one sense the goodness and badness of an action, since it derives entirely from the perceiver, is only a projection. In that sense, it is not real. It is not, for example, like the shape of an object. We think the shape is really out there in the object itself. In contrast, the appearance of wrongness or goodness is only there because the perceiver is there with his or her approval or horror.

However, there is another sense in which the moral projection is real. Most people agree with what actions are good and what actions are bad. There is consensus about which actions make us feel good – which actions are bathed in warm, inner light. For example, almost everyone would agree that acts of generosity make them feel good and acts of treachery fill them with disgust. This consensus is like the agreement that the projection is a projection of the Eiffel Tower.

The crucial point about quasi-realism is this – we can make moral mistakes under this kind of interpretation. If someone sees the Leaning Tower of Pisa when everyone else is seeing the Eiffel Tower, we can legitimately say that his or her sense of what is there has gone wrong.

Hume seems to agree with this. He talks about how we might see things in the right light. For example, we have to realize that what we see (what appearance we project) can be biased. For instance, we have to adjust for our self-interest. Perhaps the approval of slavery experienced by some people in the past could have changed had they taken into account their self-interest and their greed. Because they did not take into account the distorting filters of self-interest and narrowness of perspective, they did not cast the appropriate light onto the institution of slavery and so they made a grievous moral error. People whose perception was not biased by greed – especially the slaves themselves – did not make this error.

Conclusion

Hume is more famous as a philosopher now than he ever was in his lifetime, and he continues to inspire many modern thinkers. His legacy is huge. It is no exaggeration to say that the Western world thinks Humean thoughts and has Humean attitudes. It is as if his ideas have become part of the air we breathe. His naturalism, for example, is a crucial pillar in the cultural background of Western Europe and North America. Instead of looking towards religious ideas as a central part of our outlook, we think of the experimental method, and have a high regard for science and its ability to get to the truth.

For example, many people think of religious explanations as quaint or old-fashioned or even dangerous. This is the prevailing assumption of the so-called New Atheists such as the philosophers Richard Dawkins (1941–), Sam Harris (1967–) and Daniel Dennett (1942–). Their ideas are firmly embedded in the philosophy of the Enlightenment and Hume's naturalism. However, it is important to keep in mind that Hume himself was a sceptic. Given his naturalistic assumptions, he realized that he could not trust his faculties to deliver the truth. Reason is not the God-given ability to see into the heart of things, despite so many people's proclamations that reason can deliver truth about the world. This initially induced despair even in Hume himself, but then he regained a measure of relief from the following thought: we have no choice but to bumble along and believe the brute force of habit and custom. His philosophy is more humble than many people realize. The truth (whatever that is) might be beyond our ken, but that knowledge need not stop us in our tracks or dismay us. We may simply carry on.

Recently, some philosophers have reacted to Hume's legacy by arguing that if we can somehow regain our religious outlook, and see our faculties as shored up by God's creative power, we can also regain justified trust in the evidence of the senses (and reason and induction). In this understanding science is supported by religious assumptions rather than being antagonistic. The debate is a lively one, with the American philosophers Alvin Plantinga (1932–) being the champion of the religious option and Daniel Dennett heading up the naturalistic critics.

Hume says that morality is, to a large extent, dependent upon natural human reactions and emotions rather than being the outcome of rational reflection. This has become a large and often unnoticed part of our cultural outlook. Adverts which promote charitable giving rely more often than not on an emotional appeal. The idea that we can be argued into generosity is an option that is not often pursued. The assumption is that the truly moral person is one who has a wealth of emotional sensitivity and deep empathy towards the suffering of others. This kind of assumption is part of Hume's rich influence.

But the debate about the role of reason and emotion in morality has carried on in recent times. Emotivism, for example, claims that moral statements are entirely dependent upon emotions and can contain no truth claims at all. Some philosophers, such as Simon Blackburn (1944–), who defend quasi-realism, think we can still talk about truth in morality, but it is a truth created and sustained solely by human agreement (see Blackburn, 1993). Others want more than this. They are afraid that a morality that is wholly dependent upon human feelings is too precarious. This was the view of Hume's contemporary, Immanuel Kant (1724–1804) who was vigorous in his rejection of the role of emotion in morality. For him, true morality is a wholly rational and disinterested affair. This Kantian-inspired moral rationalism is alive and well and defended by thinkers such as Alan Gewirth (1912–2004) and Richard Hare (1919–2002). (See Gewirth, 1980 and Hare, 1952.)

Hume's suggestion that we believe in causal connections because we're habituated to expect certain events to follow others is echoed in the work of many psychologists today, who agree that our ability to track regularities gives us a working model of what to expect in many areas of our lives. Nobel prize winning psychologist Daniel Kahneman (1934–) has taken Hume's ideas of felt probabilities and turned them into experiments that show repeatedly how we have to use 'custom' or rules of thumb ('heuristics') to go about our daily lives. And Hume, says philosopher Julian Baggini (1968–), 'would not have been shocked by psychologist Daniel Kahneman's findings that the instinctive, emotional, fast thinking of the brain's "system one" usually trumps the slow, logical cogitations of "system two"' (Baggini, 2019).

The great philosopher Immanuel Kant said that Hume's works woke him from his 'dogmatic slumbers'. The founder of modern utilitarianism, Jeremy Bentham (1748–1832), said that reading Hume's works 'caused the scales to fall' from his eyes. Charles Darwin (1809–82) read Hume repeatedly during his lifetime, and regarded his work as an essential influence on his theory of evolution. Hume's six-volume *The History of England* changed the approach of written history forever, in structure, content and eminently readable tone. His work influenced the economist (and his great friend) Adam Smith, bringing about the idea of the free market which was to revolutionize world economics. And beyond all the intricate arguments of his philosophy, he reminds us constantly that we are in and of the world – we cannot descend into introspection (or reason) and expect to understand ourselves or the world around us. Allow yourself to use those rules of thumb that you have gained through everyday life, but don't believe them. Remain good-natured, but sceptical. If you choose to delve deeper into philosophy, perhaps bear in mind Hume's conclusion that,

> *'principles taken upon trust, consequences lamely deduced from them, want of coherence in the parts, and of evidence in the whole, these are every where to be met with in the systems of the most eminent philosophers, and seem to have drawn disgrace upon philosophy itself.'*
> (Hume, 1739)

Bibliography

Works by David Hume

Hume, D. (1739) *A Treatise of Human Nature*.

Hume, D. (1741, 1752a) *Essays, Moral, Political and Literary* (two parts).

Hume, D. (1748) *An Enquiry Concerning Human Understanding*.

Hume, D. (1751) *An Enquiry Concerning the Principles of Morals*.

Hume, D. (1752) *Political Discourses*.

Hume, D. (1755a) *Of Suicide*.

Hume, D. (1755b) *Of the Immortality of the Soul*.

Hume, D. (1757a) *A Dissertation on the Passions*.

Hume, D. (1757b) *Four Dissertations*.

Hume, D. (1757c) *The Natural History of Religion*.

Hume, D. (1754–62) *The History of England*.

Hume, D. (1776) *My Own Life*.

Hume, D. (1779) *Dialogues Concerning Natural Religion*.

Hume, D. (1932) *The Letters of David Hume* (2 volumes). (Edited by J.Y.T. Greig). Oxford: Clarendon Press

Other works cited

Baggini, Julian and Jenkins, Simon (2019) 'Is reason the slave of the passions?' *Prospect*, 4 May 2019.

Baggini, Julian (2018) 'Hume the humane', (ed.) Sam Dresser, *Aeon*, 15 August, 2018. Accessed Dec 2019. Available at: https://aeon.co/essays/hume-is-the-amiable-modest-generous-philosopher-we-need-today

Beebee, Helen (2012) 'Causation and Necessary Connection' in Alan Bailey and Dan O'Brien (eds.), *The Bloomsbury Companion to Hume*. London: Bloomsbury.

Blackburn, Simon (1993) *Essays in Quasi-Realism*. Oxford: Oxford University Press.

Blackburn, Simon (2003) *Being Good: A Short Introduction to Ethics*. Oxford: Oxford University Press.

Butler, Annemarie (2015) 'Hume's Early Biography and A Treatise of Human Nature' in Donald C. Ainslie and Annemarie Butler (eds.), *The Cambridge Companion to Hume's Treatise*. Cambridge: Cambridge University Press.

Craig, Edward (1987) *The Mind of God and the Works of Man*. Oxford: Clarendon Press.

Dennett, Daniel C. (2007) *Breaking the Spell*. London: Penguin.

Driver, Julia (2012) 'Hume's Sentimentalist Account of Moral Judgment' in Alan Bailey and Dan O'Brien (eds.), *The Bloomsbury Companion to Hume*. London: Bloomsbury.

Gewirth, Alan (1980) *Reason and Morality*. Chicago: University of Chicago Press.

Gopnik, A. (2009) 'Could David Hume Have Known about Buddhism?' *Hume Studies*, Vol. 35, Nos. 1 & 2, pp.5–28.

Greig, J. Y. T. (1931) *David Hume*. Oxford: Oxford University Press.

Greig, J.Y.T. (ed.) (1932) *The Letters of David Hume (2 vols)*. Oxford: Clarendon Press.

Hare, R.M. (1952) *The Language of Morals.* New York: Oxford University Press Inc.

Hutcheson, Francis (1728) *An Essay on the Nature and Conduct of the Passions, with Illustrations on the Moral Sense.* Indianapolis: Liberty Fund (this ed. 2002)

Harris, James A. (2015) *Hume: An Intellectual Biography.* Cambridge: Cambridge University Press.

Jack, Jane H. (1982), 'The Periodical Essayists' in Boris Ford (ed.), *The New Pelican Guide to English Literature: Vol. 4, From Dryden to Johnson.* Middlesex: Penguin Books.

James, William (1897), 'The Dilemma of Determinism' in *The Will to Believe and Other Essays in Popular Philosophy.* Cambridge, MA and London: Harvard University Press.

Kahnemann, D. (2012) *Thinking, Fast and Slow.* London: Penguin.

Kant, Immanuel (1948) *The Moral Law: Kant's Groundwork of the Metaphysics of Morals.* London: Hutchinson University Library.

Kenny, Anthony (2017) *The Enlightenment: A Very Brief History* London: SPCK.

De Lange, Floris and Peter Kok (2018) 'How do Expectations Shape Perception?', in *Trends in Cognitive Sciences,* June 2018.

Lowe, E.J. (2008) *Personal Agency: The Metaphysics of Mind and Action.* Oxford: Oxford University Press.

Malebranche, Nicolas (1674) 'The Search After Truth' in *The Search after Truth and Elucidations.* (Eds. Thomas M. Lennon and Paul J. Olscamp.) Cambridge: Cambridge University Press, 1997.

Mandeville, Bernard (1714) *The Fable of the Bees: Or, Private Vices, Publick Benefits.* London: Penguin Classics (this edition 1989).

Mazza, Emilio (2012) 'Hume's Life, Intellectual Context and Reception' in Alan Bailey and Dan O'Brien (eds.), *The Bloomsbury Companion to Hume.* London: Bloomsbury.

Miller, Alexander (2003) *Contemporary Metaethics: An Introduction*. Cambridge: Polity Press.

Miller, David (2003) *Political Philosophy*. Oxford: Oxford University Press.

Millican, Peter (ed.) (2002a) *Reading Hume on Human Understanding*. Oxford: Oxford University Press.

Millican, Peter (2002b) 'The Context, Aims, and Structure of Hume's First Enquiry' in Peter MIllican (ed.) *Reading Hume on Human Understanding*. Oxford: Oxford University Press.

Millican, Peter (2012) 'Hume's Scepticism about Induction' in Alan Bailey and Dan O'Brien (eds.), *The Bloomsbury Companion to Hume*. London: Bloomsbury.

Mossner, Ernest C. (1980) *The Life of David Hume (2nd edn)*. Oxford: Clarendon Press.

Murti, T.R.V. (1960) *The Central Philosophy of Buddhism*. London: George Allen & Unwin Ltd.

Norton, D. F. and Norton, M. J. (eds.) (2007) *The Clarendon Edition of the Works of David Hume: A Treatise of Human Nature, Vol. 1: Texts*. Oxford: Oxford University Press

Penelhum, Terence (2011) 'Hume's Views on Religion: Intellectual and Cultural Influences' in Elizabeth S. Radcliffe (ed.) *A Companion to Hume*. Chichester: John Wiley-Blackwell.

Plantinga, Alvin (2011) *Where the Conflict Really Lies: Science, Religion and Naturalism* Oxford: Oxford University Press.

Raphael, D. D. (ed.) (1991), *British Moralists 1650-1800*. Indianapolis: Hackett Publishing Company.

Rasmussen, Dennis C. (2017) *The Infidel and the Professor*. Princeton: Princeton University Press.

Rosen, R. (2012) *Anticipatory Systems: Philosophical, Mathematical, and Methodological Foundations*. Springer (2nd edition).

Rutherford, Donald (1995). *Leibniz and the Rational Order of Nature*. Cambridge: Cambridge University Press.

Shaftesbury (1711) *Characteristics of Men, Manners, Opinions, Times.* (3 vols). Indianapolis: Liberty Fund (this ed. 2001)

Stewart, M. A. (2005) 'Hume's Intellectual Development 1711–1752' in Martina Frasca-Spada and P. J. E. Kail (eds.), *Impressions of Hume.* Oxford: Clarendon Press.

Sturgeon, Nicholas (2011) 'Hume's Metaethics: Is Hume a Moral Noncognitivist?' in Elizabeth S. Radcliffe (ed.) *A Companion to Hume.* Chichester: John Wiley-Blackwell.

Sullivan, Roger J. (1994) *An Introduction to Kant's Ethics.* Cambridge: Cambridge University Press.

Urmson, J. O. (1982), *Berkeley.* Oxford: Oxford University Press.

Biography

Mark Ian Thomas Robson received his PhD from Durham University. His thesis was subsequently published by Continuum Press as *Ontology and Providence in Creation: Taking Ex Nihilo Seriously* (2008). Since then Mark has written a number of articles in various journals, the most recent appearing in the Royal Institute of Philosophy's journal, *Philosophy*, which explores the account of free will given by Henri Bergson. Mark teaches at a large high school in Tyne and Wear, England.

Picture Credits:

Who the hell is

This exciting new series of books sets out to explore the life and theories of the world's leading intellectuals in a clear and understandable way. The series currently includes the following subject areas:

Art History
Psychology
Philosophy
Sociology
Politics

For more information about forthcoming titles in the Who the Hell is...? series, go to **www.whothehellis.co.uk**

If any of our readers would like to put in a request for a particular intellectual to be included in our series, then please contact us at **info@ whothehellis.co.uk**

Printed in Great Britain
by Amazon